AMONG HEROES

A Marine Corps Rifle Company on Peleliu

First Sergeant Jack R. Ainsworth
United States Marine Corps

EDITED BY

AMBASSADOR LAURENCE POPE (RETIRED)

QUANTICO, VA 2011

FOREWORD

Few Americans know of the battle of Peleliu. It never received the iconic recognition of the other amphibious assaults in the Pacific during World War II such as Iwo Jima or Okinawa. At the time of the invasion in 1944, only a handful of journalists even covered the operation because it was expected to be a short action with a quick American victory. It became the bloodiest battle in Marine Corps history given the number of casualties compared to the number of troops involved. It lasted far longer than senior planners had estimated and the tenacious defense by the Japanese took a tremendous toll on the Marines' headlong assaults on their well-fortified positions.

Marines know this battle for many of the legendary figures of the Corps who fought there, including Lewis B. "Chesty" Puller, Raymond G. "Ray" Davis, and Everett P. Pope. Eight Medals of Honor, along with many other medals for heroism, were awarded in that extraordinary fight for a small coral atoll in the expansive Pacific Ocean.

It is debatable whether Americans could support and sustain the kinds of casualties that were accepted in the march across the Pacific during World War II. U.S. citizens saw the threat in those days as existential and were willing to commit all to achieve unconditional surrender. Marines had controversially asserted, decades before, that amphibious operations against fortified beaches were possible. This contradicted the accepted belief, formed after the ill-fated operation against Gallipoli in World War I. The Marines and Navy worked tirelessly during the 1920s and 30s to prove and perfect the tactics, procedures, and equipment for what is now accepted as the most complex of all military operations—the amphibious assault. Just as Marines learned more from each operation in the Pacific and refined their skills, so did the Japanese. Their tactics adjusted after each island was taken and their willingness to fight to the last man grew more intense as the American juggernaut drew closer to their homeland.

In retrospect, many of the decisions as to which islands to assault and which to bypass can be—and are—hotly debated. Even at the time, there was controversy as General Douglas MacArthur and Admiral Chester W. Nimitz saw different courses in closing on the Japanese mainland for the ultimate battle. Peleliu became central to this difference of views. Its strategic value was questionable, and questioned. It never did provide the geographic advantage that was assumed by the decision makers at the time.

History is replete with battles that were fought for questionable advantage or purpose. Some achieved legendary recognition, such as the Charge of the Light Brigade in the Crimean War. That recognition comes because of the unquestioning commitment, bravery, and sense of duty that the combatants display. At Peleliu, the Marines demonstrated their legendary courage and dogged determination to prevail.

One thing that stands out from this remarkable account of a Marine rifle company at Peleliu is the value of the Marine noncommissioned officer (NCO). We have in our Corps the lowest ratio of officers to enlisted of any service. Our tradition of a strong NCO core has served us well through 235 years of service to our country.

First Sergeant Jack R. Ainsworth's narrative epitomizes this tradition, and it exemplifies the respect, trust, and reliance we officers place in our NCOs.

Anthony C. Zinni
General, U.S. Marine Corps (Retired)

PREFACE

This narrative of six days of combat on Peleliu was discovered in my father's papers only a few months before his death on 16 July 2009. It was composed in the heat of the fighting by First Sergeant Jack Robinson Ainsworth of Company C, 1st Battalion, 1st Marines (Co C, 1st Bn, 1st Mar). My father was the company commander—the "Skipper"—to First Sergeant Ainsworth's "Top." When I showed my father the typescript, on yellowing World War II paper, he did not appear to recognize it, although the few days in the narrative had marked his life forever. Called back to active duty during the Korean War, and asked to comment on the draft of Major Frank O. Hough's official history of the battle—*Assault on Peleliu* (Washington, D.C.: U.S. Marine Corps History Division, 1950)—he made no reference to this narrative, nor did he mention it in interviews over the years, or in his 1996 oral history with the USMC History Division. The most likely explanation is that these events were so painful to recall that he set the narrative aside in his papers and then forgot about its existence. It took at least a decade after the war for his Medal of Honor to make its way slowly out of a drawer in his desk to a frame on the wall of his study.

Jack Ainsworth's account tells the story of Company C's ordeal, from the landing on 15 September to the withdrawal of its shattered remnants from the front lines five days later. It is often written in the present tense, as the fighting raged around him. How he managed to

★★★★★

take such detailed notes under these circumstances is a mystery. Ainsworth stated that he wrote on a memo pad. Did he know shorthand, perhaps? His notes must have been typed after the battle, either on the transport back to Pavuvu or at the 1st Marine Division's base. There is little sign of subsequent editing. His 56-page typescript account is marked "second copy" on the first page. The original may have been destroyed. One section on the last page was obscured when the typist forgot to insert a blank sheet under the carbon paper.

However it was composed, there can be no question about the narrative's authenticity. In virtually every respect, it accords with the detailed battle history the 1st Battalion of the 1st Marines drew up in November 1944. Where it diverges from the nearly contemporaneous official record, Ainsworth's narrative is clearly authoritative, at least with regard to the events he witnessed. The incident he recounts in which Marine tanks kill at least one member of Company C, for example, is understandably recorded nowhere else. His descriptions of the events, which resulted in the award of four Navy Crosses to men from Company C, two of them posthumous, often correct the official citations.

All other firsthand accounts of Peleliu were written well after the events they describe. Captain George P. Hunt's *Coral Comes High* (Harper & Brothers, 1946) was the first to appear. (Hunt had been a professional journalist before the war, and he makes a brief appearance in this narrative as the commanding officer of Co K, 3d Bn, 1st Mar.) Robert Leckie's *Helmet for My Pillow* (Bantam Books, 1957), Russell G. Davis's *Marine at War* (Little, Brown, 1961), and Eugene B. Sledge's *With the Old Breed at Peleliu and Okinawa* (Presidio Press, 1981), were written much later. In addition to the HBO series *The Pacific*, there is a six-foot shelf of books about the battle, the most recent of which deals solely with the ordeal of the 1st Marines.[1] Of all these accounts, Ainsworth's narrative stands out. It is one of the most harrowing and moving records of combat to survive from any theater of World War II.

First Sergeant Jack Ainsworth was born in May 1918, making him 26 in September 1944. He was older and more experienced than most of the men of Company C. He had enlisted in the Marine Corps in December 1937, and in 1940 found himself in the exotic precincts of Shanghai, where since 1927 the 4th Marines had been standing guard over the international settlement. He was a member of H Company of the 2d Battalion, and a December 1940 muster roll of that company shows that he was its lowest ranking member—he is the only private listed—and there are indications in his record that he had difficulty with authority, since he spent some time in the brig. In May 1941, a transfer stateside spared him the fate of the 4th Marines, who were evacuated from Shanghai to fight at Corregidor, enduring Japanese captivity until the end of the war. By 1943, with the rapid expansion of the Marine Corps, he quickly rose to the rank of first sergeant, and there are no further references in his record to disciplinary action. In May 1943, he shipped out from Camp Elliott, California, as a replacement to the 1st Marine Division at Melbourne, an indication that his leadership skills and experience were valued. He served with 1st Bn, 1st Mar through the Cape Gloucester campaign, and was later assigned as the first sergeant of C Co, 1st Bn, 1st Mar on Pavuvu, where the division prepared for

Jack Ainsworth enlistment photo
U.S. Marine Corps

---

[1] Richard D. "Dick" Camp, *Last Man Standing* (Minneapolis: Zenith Press, 2008).

★★★★★★

the assault on Peleliu.

His narrative is a unique portrayal of a senior Marine NCO in action. We see him taking on the traditional responsibility for bucking up a young officer overly affected by the casualties in his platoon. He looks after the men of Company C in an almost fatherly way. They are "kids," and one dead Marine is a "lad." He speaks his mind to his superiors, and his love and admiration for his fellow Marines is evident on every page. When someone has to be sent to the rear, there is no hint of criticism.

As the company first sergeant, Jack Ainsworth was responsible for running its command post, managing its communications, and accounting for its personnel to the company commander. He was thus in an ideal position to observe events at the company level. Company C is his whole world, and he is a loyalist to a fault. He is critical of other units for failing to support the company, and he dismisses the efforts of a platoon of the division's Reconnaissance Company, which had been attached to Company C too late to join in the final assault. After the company was attached to the 2d Battalion, he suggests that the commanding officer of 2d Bn, 1st Mar was prepared to fight to the last man of the 1st Battalion. That he was not alone in this is evident from the 1st Bn, 1st Mar battle history, which declares that there was "an immediate increase in morale" when the battalion was allowed to fight as a unit instead of as a "poor relation" of the 2d: "we would have followed Judas if he had been the C.O., 1st Battalion, 1st Marines."

Ainsworth's account is not only a unique combat narrative. It is also an important historical document that adds previously unknown details to our understanding of the battle itself, from the narrow but intense perspective of one rifle company of the 1st Marines. Major Hough's detailed 1950 monograph of 209 pages, the foundation for all subsequent accounts, based in part on the 1st Battalion's history of events, records laconically that on the morning of 19 September Co C, 1st Bn, 1st Mar was bogged down in a swamp facing the Umurbrogol escarpment, and that under heavy fire from automatic weapons the company withdrew from that position to attack again across a causeway on the right flank of the ridge. This is accurate as far as it goes.

What it leaves out, however, is that it was not until mid-afternoon on the 19th, after it had been pinned down under heavy fire for most of the day, unable to advance out of the swamp, that Company C was finally allowed to withdraw and reorganize for its last assault on Hill 100. When against all odds they took the position, cheered on by the battle-hardened Marines below, they were not an isolated remnant on Hill 100, as the previous accounts suggest. They had strung concertina wire to establish a perimeter, though in the words of the company commander it was "flimsy as hell," and they were resupplied during the night with grenades and even cigarettes. They maintained their lines through the night, but without reinforcements. Exposed to heavy fire from the high ground, and running out of ammunition, they could not hold the ground they had taken, and were ordered to retreat. Their command structure remained intact throughout.

Their fellow Marines were well aware of their predicament. Years later, Russell Davis wrote: "For the few men up on the higher ridge, mostly from C Company, First Battalion—it was far worse. All through the night we could hear them screaming for illumination or for corpsmen, as the Japs came at them from caves, which were all around them on the hillside. Men were hit up there and we could hear them crying and pleading for help, but nobody could help them." In this fictionalized account, Davis reconstructs a dialogue between "Lt. Mac," a naval forward observer, and an unidentified company commander:

★★★★★★

"I think we ought to get up there," he told the company commander.

"Stay put," the company commander snarled. "Those are some of my kids catching hell up there, how do you think I feel?"

He listened to the whimpering calls from the hills, and his head was down between his knees and he cursed monotonously. But he was right. We would have done them no good. (*Marine at War*, 111–12.)

As a study in military folly, the invasion of Peleliu ranks with the worst blunders of the trench warfare of World War I. As General Zinni notes in his foreword, Admiral Halsey had recommended at the last minute that Peleliu be bypassed. That clearly could have been done without risk to General MacArthur's invasion of the Philippines, but for reasons, which probably included interservice rivalry and the divided command in the Pacific, Admiral Chester W. Nimitz ordered that the assault proceed as planned. The Navy's pre-invasion bombardment was woefully inadequate. In the absence of adequate transport, almost half of the division's tanks had to be left behind. Its 155mm heavy guns were not brought ashore until D+3. (Three days after the invasion.) This forced rifle companies like Co C, 1st Bn, 1st Mar to attack heavily fortified Japanese positions with minimal support from armor or heavy artillery. "Just plain murder" was how one battalion commander at Peleliu described the frontal assault tactics they were ordered to use to attack these impregnable positions.[2]

Much of the responsibility for these tactics must lie with the commander of the 1st Marine Division, Major General William H. Rupertus—known to at least some his officers as "Rupe the Stoop." His

---

[2] The comment of LtCol Spencer S. Berger, contained in the files of Maj Frank Hough at the National Archives and Records Administration, is that "it was just plain murder to throw these battalions into the attack in that manner. I was determined that we would not be slaughtered as had been the men of 2/1 and 1/7." Berger commanded the 2d Battalion, 7th Marines at Peleliu.

orders, repeated daily, were simply that at 0800 all infantry units will resume the attack with all possible effort. When on D+6 it was clear that the gallant 1st Marines were finished, and Major General Roy S. Geiger intervened to order Rupertus to withdraw them from the front lines, Rupertus complied only after putting up what one staff officer present called "the proverbial fit." As for the legendary commander of the 1st Marines on Peleliu, Colonel Lewis B. "Chesty" Puller, it is clear that by D+5 he was no longer thinking straight.

My father's view, not objective but heartfelt, particularly in his later years, was that Colonel Puller was the principal villain of the piece. Not even his staunchest defenders would maintain that Peleliu was Chesty's finest moment, but this neglects the command responsibility of Rupertus, who was pushing Puller hard throughout.

There is some evidence that in the immediate aftermath of the battle at least my father agreed with this assessment. He had a slim volume of the anti-war poems of Siegfried Sassoon with him in the Pacific. One of them, composed in 1917, is about an affable but incompetent general. My father replaced "general" in the first line with "Rupertus," and this is his revision of the poem's last lines:

Now the Marines he smiled at are most of them dead,
And we're cursing his staff for incompetent swine.
He's a good old ___, grunted Harry to Mac,
As they slogged up to their a__³ with rifle and pack.
But he did for them both with his plan of attack.

As for Sergeant Ainsworth, he is a gung ho Marine in every fiber of his being. He has steeled himself for casualties, and he fully accepts

---

³ In the original, it is "up to Arras."

★★★★★★

that they are necessary. By the end of the narrative, however, he can no longer conceal his deep bitterness over the profligate expenditure of young lives.

Reflecting on awards after the battle, Ainsworth writes that "to name one for outstanding performance would be showing marked partiality." My father felt the same way, and he always said that he wore the Medal of Honor for the men of Co C, 1st Bn, 1st Mar.

A visitor to the National Museum of the Marine Corps outside Quantico today can hear his recorded voice say that he was not a hero, but that on Peleliu he had been among heroes. Sergeant Ainsworth's narrative is proof that he was right, at least about the second part of that statement.

Jack Ainsworth received the Silver Star for his conduct during the night of 19–20 September. The citation reads in part:

> After his company suffered heavy casualties during an assault on a strongly defended hill and was reorganizing under point-blank artillery fire, First Sergeant Ainsworth organized company headquarters and the remnants of the first and second platoons. After forming his unit, he led them to positions where they could bring direct fire to bear on hostile mortars, which were inflicting heavy casualties on our troops. He remained in the forefront of his men during enemy counterattacks, which were repelled with heavy losses to the enemy throughout the night. Always calm and aggressive, he frequently closed with the enemy in desperate hand-to-hand combat, and by his courage and coolness under fire, served as an inspiration to his men in holding the position during a perilous situation.

I have left the manuscript as First Sergeant Ainsworth wrote it, apart from corrections to obvious spelling and typing errors, and the addition of punctuation for clarity. It was a brutal war, and he writes with all the hatred he and his fellow Marines felt for their enemy. "Nipponese illegitimates" is his most polite reference to the Japanese. Some passages may shock a modern reader, but they would not come as a surprise to a veteran of the war in the Pacific. I have resisted the temptation to bowdlerize the text in any way. Occasional footnotes are added to provide context, and to explain references to the popular culture of the time.

I am grateful to Dr. Charles P. Neimeyer, director of the USMC History Division, for his support for this project, as well as to Annette D. Amerman, USMC historian, for her help in procuring First Sergeant Ainsworth's records and in identifying Marines mentioned in the narrative.

Jim Caiella of the History Division edited the manuscript with professionalism and skill. Jim created the maps—with significant help from Eric Mailander—which show the progress of C Company during the battle. Rob Kocher, also of the History Division, designed the book, which when combined with their thoughtful selection of photos from the archives, graphically illustrates First Sergeant Ainsworth's words.

Ambassador Laurence Pope (Retired)
Portland, Maine

PELELIU

Today is September 15, 1944. The time is 0300, this is D-day for the 1st Marine Division's attack on the Japanese occupied island of "Peleliu," one of many small but well-fortified islands of the Palau group in the western Carolines.

H-hour has been officially announced as 0830, which is but five-and-one-half hours before us. The troops were awake most of the night and many stayed on deck to watch the first glimpses of the naval bombardment as we draw closer to the island. Reveille at 0300 was only a reminder to the men that there remained only a few hours before we would be moving to a hostile beach.

The time is now 0315 and from where I am standing on the flag bridge, I can see the reddish-orange flashes of our big naval guns and hear the echoing report from miles across the slightly choppy sea. It is not yet light and the island of Peleliu cannot be seen except when it is occasionally silhouetted by a big explosion inland from the beach.

It is 0330 now and the troops are at breakfast, eating their scrambled eggs, bacon, coffee, and fresh fruit in the mess hall down below decks. It is still darken ship on all weather decks.

0430 and the men have finished breakfast and returned to their respective compartments to finally arrange and check their battle equipment and add a finishing touch to their weapons with brush, oil, and ramrod. These weapons are going to mean life or death in a tight spot.

On Friday, 15 September 1944, Marines climb down cargo nets from their transport to
board landing craft for the trip to White and Orange Beaches on Peleliu. In the first
three hours of the invasion, 6,000 Marines went ashore.
Defense Department Photo (Marine Corps) 117058

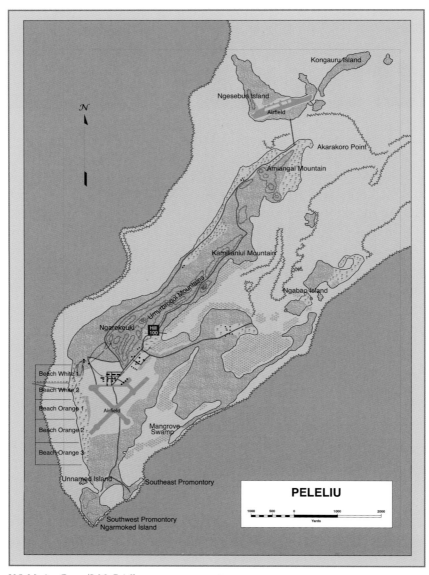

U.S. Marine Corps/J. M. Caiella

The time is now 0530 and all of C Company[4] are off the ship, some being rail loaded, others having had to climb down the big cargo nets slung over the side of the ship for that purpose. It is now 0555 and all small boats are proceeding to their pre-arranged rendezvous times. The precision and speed with which the Navy riggers and boat crews worked in disembarking troops into the LCVPs [Landing Craft, Vehicle, Personnel] was well worth seeing. They know their jobs and do them well.

Technical Sergeant [Don H.] Bauer is remaining aboard the ship to keep watch over the extra gear that the men are leaving behind. Bedding rolls, lower packs, and excess equipment will be brought ashore after a beachhead has been established and we move inland.

It is light enough now to see the island and most of our fleet as well. There are six battleships in sight, about five or six heavy and light

---

[4] 1stSgt Ainsworth also referred to Company C as C Company Charlie Company, and C/1/1. He also used the latter style in referencing other units, such as Company K, 2d Battalion, 1st Marines as K/2/1.

cruisers, numerous destroyers and an uncountable number of LCIs [Landing Craft, Infantry] and smaller craft. All these are shelling the beaches and inland targets. At present, the only aircraft overhead are Navy observation planes, which number five at this time.

The time is now 0622, the sky is overcast and the beaches are under a heavy air bombardment and naval barrage. There are several huge columns of black smoke billowing skyward from different points on the island. We are still circling in rendezvous with four other LCVPs, which compose half of Wave 13. I am writing this account of the landings sitting on the engine housing of LCVP No. 75, which is tossing around like a matchstick in the rough water.

I wish I could see everything at once, this is really a spot for a *LIFE* magazine photographer and a newspaper reporter. Barnum and Bailey only had a sideshow in comparison to this one. A direct hit was scored on a fuel or ammunition dump at 0629 and the flames must have shot upwards of 200 feet, black smoke puffing up from the target in great gusts. 0632 and here come our planes. About nine or ten different flights of torpedo planes, dive-bombers, and fighter-bombers are flying at about 8,000 feet and are directly over the island, coming in fast from a southwesterly direction. The leading formation is starting to peel off in a wingover and dive on targets. Other formations of planes are

A portion of Peleliu is obscured by smoke as naval gunfire and supporting air units prepare the island for the invasion forces. Assault craft from the first wave are forming up for the run to the beach.
Defense Department Photo (Marine Corps) 94875

now coming in on station and the air strikes are on.

The time is now 0638 and the bombing and shelling is continuing in all its fury. We are still in rendezvous and more small boats are proceeding to their rendezvous areas. 0647 and the island is nearly enveloped in smoke; the battleships and cruisers are pounding hell out of everything the observation plane asks them to. Ngesebus Island to our left is also under attack by our planes, although not as heavily as is Peleliu.

The time is now 0711. The men in my boat are very calm and composed, stretched out on deck, packs off and taking it easy, so easy in fact that they are a bit annoying. The only one who seems the least bit nervous besides myself is "Bruce," the messenger dog who is seasick and has vomited several times up to now. At this stage of the operation, everything has been just as it was at our dress rehearsal at Tassafaronga, on Guadalcanal. We have received very little return fire up to this time. Peleliu is under a blanket of smoke and dust as the bombardment rages on. Still no enemy air opposition is being encountered by our air force and very little antiaircraft fire. It seems impossible that anything could possibly remain alive under this terrific air and naval bombardment but we will know how effective this bombardment has been when we get on the beach.

It is now one hour and 13 minutes before the first waves start moving in on the beach. Our three waves should land one hour afterward (0930–0940). The Navy told us yesterday aboard ship that within 48 hours we will have contributed another chapter to the glorious history of the Marine Corps. "We hope it is not another chapter like Tarawa."[5]

---

[5] Ainsworth's reference to Tarawa is an indication of the foreboding he and the men felt. In a pre-invasion pep talk, MajGen Rupertus told the men that it would be a short and sharp action, lasting three or four days, and that it would resemble the landing on Tarawa by the 2d Marine Division in November 1943. Perhaps he thought that this would fill them with a desire to emulate the 2d Division's conduct at Tarawa, but the reference was not well calculated to inspire them with confidence. An account of the carnage at Tarawa and photographs of dead Marines on the beach published in the 13 December 1943 issue of *LIFE* magazine had shocked the home front.

★★★★★★

The time is now 0730. The southwestern part of Peleliu is totally obscured by smoke and it is one hour before the troops start to land. The entire ocean as far as the eye can see is a myriad of ships, boats, and barges and wreckage from beach defenses and destroyed Nipponese craft. Our ships and planes are really giving them plenty of hell now. Dante's Inferno is comparable to an Ice Follies when it comes to having a hot time. This is really HOT.

It is 0830 now, H-hour is here and from my position I can clearly see the first wave of the invasion heading in at a fast clip toward the beach. There is return fire meeting our landing boats now as they near the coral reef, which extends about 400 yards out in the water from the sandy beach. The water is shallow over the coral ledge and the amph-tracks[6] are openly exposed to any type of fire the enemy care to register on us. I think the Nips fully realize their advantage now and they're really pouring it on us with artillery, mortar, and machine gun fire as we get in close to the jumping off point. We hope the first waves don't run into much after they clear the tractors and hit the beach, but at the same time I'm afraid it's going to be plenty rough going the way the shells are falling at present. Geysers of water are jumping up all around our ships now but our bombardment continues, increasing in intensity. Arriving on the scene are more and more planes, relieving those who have expended all bombs and ammunition, some of the planes are dropping "NAPOM" [napalm] which is burning up anything it touches. This is really a show of shows.[7]

The time is now 0857 and we have moved out of rendezvous and up to the line of departure where we will transfer to LVTs for the landing. 0905, we're coming into the transfer area now and all men have their gear on and are standing up in the boat taking in everything. 0911, the amph-tracks just blew up from enemy fire and are burning badly.

---

[6] LVT (Landing Vehicle, Tracked). Ainsworth also refers to them as tractors.
[7] *The Show of Shows* (1929) was a lavish revue film, which featured most of the contemporary Warner Brothers film stars.

One of our planes is coming down in flames over the island. The Nips are throwing everything they have at us now, but we've got to get on that beach. Jap mortar fire is falling everywhere on the beach and just off the beach in the shallow water where the men have to get out of the tractors and wade in. I imagine the casualties are going to be fairly high for the first few waves, but perhaps the enemy will withdraw from the immediate defenses of the beach, and if so we'll have a chance to get organized and start a push.

We are still too far out to see plainly if there is any hand-to-hand fighting on the beach but if there is, we will be in it before too long. It is now 0923 and we are in the process of transferring to LVTs. 0928 and we are now moving in to the beach to support the waves already there. Mortar shells are starting to drop in front of my tractor now and are getting closer as we move in. They're dropping all around us now and the gunners on the tractor's machine guns are yelling at the men to keep down low and also giving us the dope on how much further we have to get. Three more tractors full of men just blew up on the right of mine. 0940 and we are on the coral reef. It won't be long now.

It is 0945 now and all C Company is ashore. The beach is sharp jagged coral, with coral cliffs in some places up to 12 feet in height. The men in my tractor got out of the water okay and made for a coral cliff that hung out over the water, offering a little protection until we are able to locate our forward CP [Command Post]. We had to wade in from where our tractor stopped along with stumbling and crawling over the sharp coral heads and through much barbed wire to the protecting coral cliffs. There are too many men in this area and one mortar shell could do a helluva lot of damage. We are mixed in with the 2d Battalion command post and Captain [Albert J.] Rach, the company executive officer, has taken off with a runner to find the position of our battalion relative to where we are at present. We are definitely too far to the right. The tractors have landed us on the wrong beach. What a war.

From our position under the cliffs we can see Marines being blown to bits by mortar and artillery fire and our own tractors being blown out of the water and burning the occupants alive. This may be another TARAWA. Our runner has returned and is guiding us to our company assembly area.

Engaged in the bitter struggle to establish the Peleliu beachhead, Marine infantrymen carry on the fight from the shelter of an amphibious tractor that brought them ashore. Note the *nom de guerre* of the tractor.
Headquarters U.S. Marine Corps 85253

C Company has already suffered casualties, First Lieutenant

After getting off the rugged coral beach, Marines moved into Japanese-dug tank traps as they moved forward into an area of brush and sparse coconut groves.
Defense Department Photo (Marine Corps) 102047

[Raymond W.] Mueller having been shot and killed just a few seconds after alighting from his tractor. Sergeant [Austin M.] Wortley was badly wounded by the same sniper that killed Lieutenant Mueller.[8] Pharmacists Mate Third Class [Edward H.] Auerbach suffered the same fate as the lieutenant when attempting to reach him and render aid. Private First Class John H. Brown took enemy shrapnel in two places through his right shoulder and is at present awaiting evacuation. Sergeant Mike Matyas was wounded in the left hand by shrapnel and is likewise waiting to be evacuated under his own protests. These casualties occurred between 0945 and 1130.

The company is now well off the rugged coral beach and is occupying deep tank traps formerly used by the Japanese. The surrounding area is partially coconut grove and low, thick brush. In numerous places the yellow sands are stained red with the blood of Marines already down in battle. Strangely enough, no one has seen any dead Japs excepting the one sniper, which killed our lieutenant and corpsman. He was liquidated by flamethrower and demolition charges under the supervision of Sergeant Charles [R.] Monarch's assault team.

It is now 1300 and we are moving our position about 200 yards to

---

[8] Sgt Wortley was badly wounded but survived. His dog tag was recovered on White Beach in 1996 by Eric Mailander.

our left and about 100 yards further in from the beach, digging in and disappearing at the bottom and halfway up the seaward side of a small coral ridge. Our 60mm mortar observation post is now situated on the crest of this ridge and is in plain view of the enemy airfield. Our mortars are set up in the rear of the company headquarters and part of the third platoon and machine gun platoons form the defensive line for the night and are on the forward slope of our ridge. The mortar OP [Observation Post] is in visual contact with both platoons on the line and will be able to direct mortar fire effectively in front of them if a major breakthrough starts. The 2d Battalion has the main line of defense with the 1st Battalion as a secondary line. Both lines, however, are very flimsy. Enemy mortars continue to drop in this area and frequent screams for corpsmen are to be heard. Lieutenant Stanford of the Naval Forward Observer Service and Private First Class [Ignatz J.] Matello were both slightly wounded by mortar shrapnel, though not seriously, and they are both sticking it out with the company.

The time is now 1700. The mortar OP has just called down to us that there are eight Japanese tanks starting to cross the airfield in our direction. There is a gap or saddle at both the right and left flanks of the ridge we are dug in behind, and those gaps are being filled with men and machine guns and one armored amph-track in case the Nips try an attack at either of these points. Captain [Everett P.] Pope, the company commander, has called for a bazooka team to further strengthen the weak points.

I have just finished a conversation with Major [Nikolai] Stevenson[9] over the telephone informing him of the present situation. His words were to keep a stiff upper lip on the line and knock them out if we get the chance. There are three Sherman tanks now moving out on the strip to meet the Jap tankettes. The tankettes are hesitating at present but

---

[9] Maj Stevenson, who had previously been the CO of C/1/1, was the executive officer of 1/1.

now they are coming on again. Our Shermans are firing their 75mms as fast as the gunner can load and sight. Three Nip tankettes have been hit already and are out of action and are burning hotly on the airfield. Here come two dive-bombers and are shooting rockets at the remaining Jap tanks. And what an aim those flyers have! They have knocked out two more of the tankettes.

Private First Class [Dominic A.] Vittetta and Corporal [Jerrold L.] Edwards have moved forward to within range of the closest enemy tank, which is trying to get through our lines. They are going to take it out with their bazooka and they have hit it already. They have hit it on the side and the tank has stopped. They are sighting in again and this time they have torn the turret completely off the tank. Those boys have what it takes and plenty of it. Oddly enough, everyone on the line has stopped thinking about the war for just enough time to take in the tank and bazooka battle. The two remaining Jap tanks are now in disorderly retreat back across the airstrip and our tanks are in hot pursuit.

I have reported the results of the battle to Major Stevenson and he is happy over the outcome and I rather imagine somewhat relieved. I know damn well everybody up here is. As a result of the action against the enemy tanks, Private First Class Gordon Davidson [Jr.] has been wounded badly in the back of the head by a piece of shrapnel which ricocheted off the side of the tank and into his foxhole. He is being evacuated immediately but it is very doubtful whether or not he will live to reach the ship and receive proper surgery. Little Davey is the baby of the company, we all hope for the best.[10] It is getting too dark to write anymore, and all hands are puffing on their last cigarette for today. Hope all goes well tonight and that we see another dawn. It is now 1805 and the total casualties for today are two killed, six wounded. We have gotten off lightly considering everything. Good night.

---

[10] PFC Davidson survived thanks to his friend PFC Arthur Simpson, who carried him back to the beach. Simpson was wounded the next day by friendly fire (see 17 September 1944).

The hills around Umurbrogol Mountain are silhouetted by star shells, tracers, and explosions during night fighting on Peleliu.
Headquarters U.S. Marine Corps 100821

16 SEPTEMBER 1944

★★★★★★

The time is now 0634. All during the night the entire island was kept illuminated by mortar flares and Navy star shells. Both the hostile and the friendly firing kept up through the hours of darkness, and several times it sounded as though an enemy counterattack had started. However, each time the firing increased in intensity, it died out within a few moments to sporadic bursts of machine gun and automatic weapons fire. I kept in direct communication with Major Stevenson throughout the night by telephone, passing on any information available from the mortar OP above us.

We suffered no casualties during the night, but apparently the Japs have infiltrated our lines because everyone has just hit the deck and are firing into the brush and trees. Where the target is, I'm sure I don't know. We are even firing into our own lines.

The time is 0700. The firing has ceased now and the men are getting on their feet again and looking in the direction of the battalion command post. The phone is ringing. I answer to Major Stevenson telling him what little I know of the last foray and am told that they have killed two Nips in the immediate vicinity of the [battalion] CP. There is no more firing in our area.

As a result of the anti-sniper action, Private First Class [Murray L.] Ball was hit in the leg by small-arms fire and has been removed to the battalion aid station. It has just been reported to me that Privates First

★★★★★★

Class [John J.] Maguire and [Dale D.] Byrd[11] have been missing since yesterday. They were last seen on the beach shortly after landing, pinned down by sniper fire.

The time is now 0730 and another naval and air bombardment has begun, moving from .01 to .02,[12] and covering every square yard of ground within these bounds. When the barrage lifts and moves on .02, the 2d and 3d Battalions, reinforced by B Company, 1st Battalion, will attack .02. It has just been reported to me that Corporals [Jerrold L.] Edwards and assistant cook [Jennings F.] Harvey were both wounded by shrapnel. Edwards is sticking it out with the company, but Harvey has been evacuated to a ship.

The time is now 1047 and we are still in the position we occupied last night, awaiting order[s] committing us in the attack. Sergeant Monarch with his assault team was called upon by the 3d Battalion to demolish a cave where some Japs are keeping operations held up by withering machine gun fire. Monarch and his team employed a flamethrower as a starter and finished it off with a nice large charge of C-2 composition. Our flamethrowers are now being recharged and more ammunition is being distributed to those who want or need it.

The time is now 1215 and Charlie Company has taken up attack formation practically on the beach in a sandy shell-torn coconut grove. This is our first time to be committed in this operation and we are on the scene where a tank and artillery duel was raging just one hour ago. Many dead Marines litter the area we are assembl[ed] in and likewise many Japs. I feel a bit ashamed mentioning dead Japs in the same sentence with Marines, but that is the exact picture as I see it. Marines and Japs, sprawled over one another giving evidence of death struggles where both had been caught in machine gun fire and crumpled in a misshapen heap of limbs and entrails on the already red sand. Mortar

---

[11] PFC Emery A. Byrd Jr. was wounded the following day.
[12] Map phase lines. See map, p. 36.

and artillery fire leave its victims in horrible grotesque positions, partially decapitated, minus limbs, and sometimes fully draped in their own intestines. It's hard to believe even when you see it with your own eyes.

The time is now 1220. The barrage is lifting and moving considerably ahead of us, depositing tons of white-hot steel and explosives on the enemy who is resisting stiffly between phase lines .01 and .02. There is much machine gun and rifle fire being directed into the seaward slope of a low, but rugged, coral ridge that runs parallel to the beach and is on our right flank. We are also receiving automatic weapons fire from pillboxes and coral caves as well as mortar fire.

A rumor has started circulation that Able and Baker Companies have been hit hard, suffering a lot of casualties. It is only a rumor, however, and has yet to be confirmed. I might take this time to say that we have encountered damned stiff resistance all the way, which I can add is not very far.

The time is now 1224 and Charlie Company is waiting for the word "GO." Planes are on the set now and are dive bombing and strafing targets between the aforementioned phase lines. This harasses the enemy somewhat, but we know that the lousy bastards will have to be

Waiting for the green light, Marines are ready to clear a small ridge to face the enemy on the other side.
Headquarters U.S. Marine Corps 95602

After landing nearly one full beach south of their designated point, Company C was held in reserve the first day and committed to action the next. Their movement paralleled the beach until turning inland where they confronted a blockhouse on the third day.

Headquarters U.S. Marine Corps 95256

★★★★★★

rooted out by cold steel, one-by-one, or sealed up in their caves by the score if an opportunity presents itself to us.

The time, 1230, and here we go. The first platoon on the right, second platoon on the left, third platoon in support, two squads of machine guns in the rear of third platoon, and company headquarters bringing up the rear. The mortars remaining in the area we are jumping off from [are] to fire over our heads when called upon. The OP is up ahead on the front lines with Lieutenant Currier in charge of the 81s and Lieutenant Peck spotting for the Charlie Company 60s. Our men are now moving ahead at a steady pace and there is alertness and caution in every step taken. They know that the area through which they are now passing is heavily mined and a misstep means curtains or crippled for life. Not only are they watching where they put their feet down, but [they] keep their eyes peeled for snipers in the trees, in spider traps, and pillboxes, which might conceal a Nip playing possum.[13]

As we advance, the picture looks somewhat like this: First Lieutenant [Walter] Shaffner[14] has his platoon deployed on a skirmish line extending from the base of the ridge on the seaward side to the left and over the deep trenched sandy coconut grove. The man on the extreme left of his platoon marks the left flank of the company with no contact with any other unit at this time. Lieutenant [Francis T. "Frank"] Burke is tied in with Lieutenant Shaffner's right flank and his platoon is deployed up the side of the ridge, over the top and down on the island side finally stretching out into some flat but heavily wooded ground and in physical contact with K Company, 3d Battalion, on his right.[15]

The area through which we are now passing is rutted with deep

---

[13] The 1950 monograph compiled by Maj Hough for the USMC History Division describes this attack as follows: "The regimental reserve (1st Battalion) attacked strongly in the early afternoon, with Company C the last fresh element in assault and one platoon of Company B in reserve. Two tanks had been brought up, and with their support the infantry succeeded in capturing a 500-yard segment of the ridge" (Hough, 74).

[14] A posthumous recipient of the Navy Cross. (See 19 September 1944 entry).

[15] K/3/1 was commanded by Capt George Hunt. They had landed on the extreme left of White Beach, and been ordered to attack fortified Japanese positions on the point that,

tank traps and enemy communication trenches, to say nothing of many pillboxes that are constructed of coconut logs and camouflaged with sand and brush, making them nearly invisible until you are practically standing on top of them. Once in a predicament like this, very little can be done to alleviate your misfortune, therefore it is what is known as a most embarrassing situation. However, the men have a slightly different way of putting it, which I believe is "TS." The abbreviation could mean Tough Situation or Terrible Spot, but it doesn't.

The time is now 1430 and my CP is located approximately 75 yards in rear of the assault platoons in a big tank trap just to the left of a road, which lies at the base of and parallel to the ridge already thrice mentioned. Doubtless we have suffered some casualties thus far in the attack but it is too early to receive word of them yet. I have Captain Pope's spam-can radio and I'm able to keep in contact with the front line by relaying messages through a set in the hands of Lieutenant Currier up at the 81mm mortar OP.[16] Lieutenant Shaffner has just contacted me and has asked me to get water, and all types of small arms ammunition up to him as soon as possible. I assured him that all he asked for was already on the way up and should be at his CP any moment.

I am in command of the company command post and I can say that my kids are surely doing a swell job of getting the necessary water and ammunition up to the lines as well as bearing litter when casualties occur. None of them have time to sit down or rest. If they're not on the way to the front lines with field messages, they are taking one to the

---

virtually untouched by the naval bombardment, threatened the entire landing. Company K was decimated in this epic action, cut off and reduced at one point to 18 men, but Hunt and his men held their ground against determined counterattacks, and finally managed to link up with B and C Companies. By this time, of the 235 men who had landed, there were only 78 left. (Capt Hunt, who received the Navy Cross, described this action in his book *Coral Comes High* [1946]. A journalist before the war, he later became managing editor of *LIFE* magazine.) In his oral history with the USMC History Division, Pope recalls establishing contact with Hunt's company.

[16] The primitive SR-536 Handie Talkie or "spam can" radio had limited range. Communications over even short distances were often difficult or impossible, as 1stSgt Ainsworth's account makes clear, and he often had to relay messages between the company commander and battalion.

battalion at the rear.

The front lines are now calling frantically for corpsmen and stretchers. They have run into white-hot hell on the nose of the ridge. We are getting withering automatic fire from a pillbox right on the point of the ridge we are extended over. It is reinforced steel and concrete and it sounds like 40mm or 60mm guns firing from the embrasures. Until we can knock out this strongpoint, it's a solid cinch that we won't get anywhere and right now I'm given to say, "We are definitely not winning this war."

The damn Japs held their fire until we got within practically point-blank range of their guns and then opened up with everything including supporting mortar fire. Their well-camouflaged position made it impossible to detect the fate awaiting our boys as they came out of the brush and into the open.

It is now 1657 and it seems only a few moments ago that we jumped off in the attack. The immediate problem at hand is obtaining and installing barbed wire as part of the night's defensive set up ahead of the lines. If we don't get the barbed wire in before dark, anything can happen and probably will. The bastards have all the high ground and can observe without strain every move we make.

The battalion CP has just called me on the radio and has ordered me to pull our company command post back about 50 yards and tie in with them for the night. It is now 1708 and we have moved back to where battalion is and are tying in with them as ordered. Barbed wire and more ammunition is now going past the CP and into the front lines, which makes all hands feel a little better. A demolitions crew from the 17th Marines are roaming through the command post area and are setting charges of explosives in all partly demolished dugouts and pill boxes, making sure that no live Japs are within our lines before darkness.

There are many dead Marines throughout our entire layout but we have no time to bury them. The best we can do at present is to cover them up with ponchos or shelter halfs and wait for burial parties to come along and do the job properly. I particularly noticed one corpse, a lad of about 17 or 18 years of age, sprawled forward in the sand face down and eyes closed as if he had fallen asleep in the sun. Although the pallor of death was on his face, he was one of the few Marines who died quickly and without being mutilated by shell fire. Just a dark red stain coming from the underside of his body and having run out onto the sand gave evidence that he had been shot cleanly through the heart. His hands were clenched tightly holding a bit of the bright yellow sand in their grasp. The terrific heat was already starting to bloat the bodies

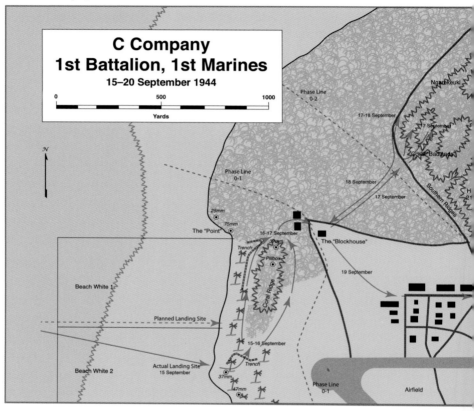

and the odor of death hang[s] heavily over the area like a mist, but to many who died here, death was doubtless an angel of mercy, freeing them from agonizing pain and the misery of leading a future life, a hopeless, helpless cripple.

It is now 1800 and I'll take this opportunity to say that the quartermaster department of the 1st Battalion have done a bang up job. They are masters of the problem of supply and our hats are off to them,

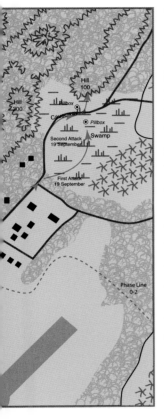

but not for long. No sir, a guy is just a plain "umpchay" to take that old helmet off and keep it off for any length of time in this war. My company gunnery sergeant [George W. Pyles] is in the process of brewing a cup of coffee, C-ration type, over a small chunk of composition C-2. Although this soluble coffee will take the hair off your teeth, it's mighty stimulation to the system. What system I hesitate to say, but at any rate it's a hot drink and we will feel better after a cup or two.

I have just finished a conversation with Lieutenant Burke of C Company in person. His platoon has had three killed and four wounded during this afternoon's attack and he feels badly about it. I cheered him up as best I could with due respect for state of mind and offered my condolences, knowing all of the men personally, having been their top kick for many months.

Lieutenant Burke is doing a wonderful job in what is his baptism of fire, but letting your number of casualties get you down is one thing we have to guard against. It should make us fight all the more savage when we learn of our best buddies getting cut down by those lice-ridden baboons who live in caves, eat rice, and call themselves human. But we "WILL TAKE THIS ISLAND" no matter what. Darkness has pounced on us and it is again too dark to continue writing so I'll secure until morning and hope that all goes well during the night. The time is 1842.[17]

---

[17] Despite the hard push, at the end of D+1 Charlie Company and the rest of the battalion had been stopped some 200 to 300 yards short of the road, which marked the .02 phase line.

Company C made an abortive foray into the southern coral ridges on 17–18 September, and two attempts at taking Hill 100 on the 19th.
U.S. Marine Corps

19 Sept
084

Hill 100

19 September
1615

17-18 September

• CP

17 September

L Company

3 Stacks

18 September   17 September

17

★ ★ ★ ★ ★ ★
SEPTEMBER 1944

As I awake and look at my watch, the time is 0545. The companies kept up the attack all during the night, giving the Nips no more chance to sleep than we had. There were two companies within our command post last night and early this morning.

At about 2330 last night, Private First Class Fonda, a messenger dog handler, stood up in his foxhole to stretch his legs and change position. He was immediately challenged by another Marine a few yards away and failed to answer the password, crouching back in his hole. The Marine, whose name we will not mention, promptly attacked with cold steel. Over the edge of the foxhole he went and jumped into the hole he thought [was] occupied by a Jap. His knife slashed into the back of the Marine several times before he discovered it was one of our own men. Fonda was evacuated immediately to the battalion aid station and the attacker was calmed down and put at ease by his buddies and congratulated on his determination to keep the enemy out of our positions regardless of the mistaken identity. It was the fault of Fonda, not the man who challenged. Lessons like this sink in and are long remembered. Word has reached us that PFC Fonda is not in a serious condition, although his wounds are painful, he will pull through O.K.[18]

Again, at 0315 this morning, Corporal Arthur Simpson Jr. was shot through the left shoulder by fire from within our own lines. Simpson was evacuated at daybreak, not in a critical condition. Another lesson

---

[18] PFC Fonda is not listed as having been wounded in action.

that it does not pay to move around after darkness out of your foxhole. Stay that way and remain intact.

Orders have been received to commence the attack again at 0800. All hands are awake now and shaking the sand out of their clothes and brushing off their weapons in preparation for the new assault. After eating more C rations for a breakfast, all men have replenished their ammunition supply and filled their canteens with fresh water. Water is hard to get and the men are cautioned against wasting it or drinking too much at a time. It is a dark color and tastes very much like crude oil, but it's water and the doctors have okayed it for drinking so we've no kick coming.[19]

It is now 0800 and we are moving up fast in the attack on the nose of the ridge to knock out the pillbox that has already caused so much damage to us. It is 0819 and the guns in that pillbox are no longer spitting lead. The gunners must be dead or hit badly enough to be counted

---

[19] The barrels brought ashore for drinking water had been used to store oil and had not been adequately cleaned. The water was virtually undrinkable, adding to the suffering of the men and the cases of heat exhaustion. In 1stSgt Ainsworth's "we've got no kick coming," the voice of the first sergeant telling the men to suck it up is audible.

as out of action. The demolitions crew are placing a big load of C-2 in the back door of this monkey cage and they are yelling "fire in the hole," meaning to look out below, she's going up. And up it goes; concrete, coral, Japs, machine guns, and ammunition. It has been definitely neutralized and is out of our way, allowing us to race through the narrow pass and into an area where many new laid concrete foundations have been torn up by our shelling and bombing. We are hell bent for .02, and the way we're rolling now, it'll take a damn good army to stop us. "A damn good army."

It is 0835 and we are advancing on a huge concrete-and-steel blockhouse. This looks to be the size of a modern two-story hotel, which would have about 40 rooms with baths. There is very little resistance in this area and some of our men are already climbing atop the formidable structure. Others are running up to the sides of this fort and throwing grenades in through the shell holes, which can be counted on the fingers of one hand. The walls of this strong point are at least four feet in thickness and are reinforced every six inches with one-half-inch steel rods running both horizontally and vertically. Our naval shelling and aerial bombardment have hardly marked this giant bastion, yet all resistance from the interior of it has ceased.

A few of the men with possibly a bit more curiosity than others are moving up to the entrance. The doors of solid steel are ajar and we are anxiously awaiting what results the men will get when they throw in several grenades. In go the grenades and the men duck around the corners for protection from shrapnel. Wham! go the grenades, and in go a bunch of Marines, tommy guns blazing a path in front of them. A few more bursts and the show is over inside. One Marine runs out and waves "all clear." The mighty blockhouse is ours. The men are swarming over the surrounding landscape toward the newly won prize, if it

An M-4 Sherman tank rumbles past the ruins of the concrete and steel blockhouse, which Company C encountered on the third day of the invasion. The Japanese machine shop became the Marines' battalion aid station and command post.
U.S. Marine Corps

★★★★★★

can be so considered. A few moments are taken to check against booby traps and land mines, and we continue the attack toward .02. The big blockhouse will soon house the battalion aid station and command post, giving a great feeling of security to those within.[20]

We are fully in the attack now and I have just receipted for a message that Lieutenant Shaffner's platoon is in their section of .02. The time is now 0910 and the rest of the company is coming up on line with Lieutenant Shaffner's platoon. We need stretchers and bearers badly now as we are at the foot of one of the highest hills on the island and the Japs are dropping their mortar shells right down on top of us. .02 is right at the edge of a built-up coral road and is a perfect registration point for enemy artillery and mortar fire. They are using both now with a very high degree of effectiveness. Men are falling faster than the corpsmen can get them on stretchers and patch them up.

I'm calling battalion on the telephone now and expect to get Major Stevenson any second. The major answered the phone himself and I explained to him just what the situation is and how badly

Marines engage in their daily routine at an infantry battalion command post, not unlike the one with which the author communicated.
Headquarters U.S. Marine Corps 9707

---

[20]USMC historian Maj Hough reported this massive blockhouse was protected by 12 pill-boxes, mutually supporting and connected by tunnels, and had been completely missed by the pre-invasion bombardment although it was visible on aerial photographs. (The naval task force commander, RAdm Jesse B. Oldendorf, famously declared before the invasion that he had run out of targets.) After the war, the admiral told Maj Hough that much of his staff had been in sickbay. It is safe to say that this excuse would not have impressed the 1st Marines. By 0930, the battalion CP was established in the blockhouse, "with about 20 freshly dead Japanese" (Hough, 79–80). Sgt Charles R. Monarch received the Navy Cross for his part in this action. The citation states that he "personally placed heavy explosive charges into the embrasures, destroying ten of the stronghold."

we are in need of corpsmen and stretchers.[21] We are continuing to be plastered by enemy shellfire and our casualties are mounting by the minute. The first ones hit are being brought back past the command post on their way to the rear where the battalion aid station is now located. They are in pretty bad shape. One of them said to me in passing, "It's those God-damned mortars again, Top. Every time we move they open up. Where in Christ's name is our artillery? Can't someone do something about those mortars. They'll get us all before it's over."

Artillery action against those mortars right now would be a complete waste of ammunition and couldn't even be used as harassing fire. The enemy mortars are dug in on the reverse slope of the hill in front of us, and our artillery shells would only pass harmlessly over them to explode in some swamp or unimportant target. What we need now is counter-battery fire with 81s and dive-bombing of the Nip mortar positions.

It is now 1058 and our planes apparently have received orders to start an air strike for there are many carrier-based planes circling over us at this moment. Casualty reports have not started to reach me as yet, but I know there will be many more this morning and still more as they day wears on. Amphibian tractors are bringing up water, some fruit juices, C rations, stretchers and stretcher bearers, and evacuating the wounded on their return. It has been several hours since the second platoon reached .02 and now the entire company is on this phase line.

The time is now 1300 and the command post is moving up to a point approximately 50 yards in rear of our company front. We have just received orders to attack .03 at 1400.

The heat on this island is terrific and is taking its toll of men by heat exhaustion. Gunnery Sergeant Pyles is suffering from the intense heat and has been ordered to stay behind when we move out and join us

---

[21] Wire had been strung to permit telephone communications between Charlie Company and the battalion CP.

★★★★★★

after he has recuperated sufficiently. Captain Rach is also sick and is a bit delirious as a result of a head injury sustained on D-day when he was felled to his knees by a huge piece of coral hitting him on top of the head. Had the captain not been wearing his helmet he would have been killed instantly. The coral came from a cave that was being blown up by our demolition crew.

It is 1545 now and only 15 minutes until we push the attack toward .03. We are moving up to the coral road and on line with the company. We are going to have a very narrow front at the beginning of this attack so the platoons will move out in echelon: the first platoon in the assault, the second in support, the third in reserve, two squads of machine guns also in reserve, and company headquarters on the tail end as always. The mortars are not on this push, but have been assigned an area about 500 yards up the road to a point where he can more effectively put the 60s to use should we need that type of fire.

The planes that have been above us for some time are now raining bombs down on targets in the ravine, which we will enter in about ten minutes. The planes are doing plenty of strafing but I don't believe they come in low enough to gain the maximum effect—strafing from 2,000 feet is merely harassing fire and the bullets are too widely dispersed by the time they hit the earth to even come close to the target the pilot saw through his sights in the plane. What we really need is about four squadrons of Marine [F4U] Corsairs. They come in so low on their strafing missions the pilot's hip pockets dip sand when he pulls out and banks to the left or right.

The time is 1400 and here we go ahead, over the coral road and into the thick underbrush, which covers the bottom of the ravine between two steep ridges [that] rise probably 100 feet above our present level. Captain Rach has passed completely out of the picture and is being

A camouflaged LVT-4 carrying a Navy MK 1 flamethrower attacks a Japanese position on Peleliu. Four of the modified LVTs were provided to the 1st Marine Division for the invasion, and were in the first wave, one on each White Beach.
Headquarters U.S. Marine Corps 98260

carried to the rear. Private First Class [Virgil W.] Clemmer has already been hit and is being pulled out of the fight. There is a Navy amph-track with flamethrower attached up ahead of us in the attack and it is roasting the Nips alive in their caves.

The advance has slowed down and we are barely moving at all. The captain is up ahead with the assault platoon as usual. This valley, or ravine as I labeled it previously, is honeycombed with caves, dugouts, and just plain holes where the Nips are putting up fairly stiff resist-ance.[22] As we advance, we pass large caches of Japanese supplies of all types—food, ammunition, medical supplies, rubber goods (not the kind found in a Marine's wallet), and various other heaps of junk—all of which must be bypassed as much as we'd all like to rummage through it for souvenirs.

A runner has just come up to me and handed me a message from the company commander. It reads, "First Sergeant Ainsworth, pull company headquarters back down the ravine to the road and meet me

[22] A post-invasion survey put the total number of caves on Peleliu at more than 500 (Hough, 194–195).

★★★★★★

with your men about eight hundred yards up the coral road, make it fast." Signed CO-C/1/1.

I have rogered for the message and am pulling out of the ravine as ordered. On our way out we passed the 17th Marines demolitions crew who have received orders to destroy all caves, pillboxes, and supply dumps in this area and to blow up all antipersonnel and antitank mines they come across. Just upon reaching the coral road at the mouth of the ravine, KA WHAM! And looking back into the ravine we can still see Japs [and] debris of all sorts still going up, up, up, in the air. What a charge they must have dropped in on Tojo's boys that time. Dirt and small pieces of coral are dropping on us now as the echo of the explosion is dying out up the ravine.

Company headquarters is in a single file on both sides of the road and moving up at a fast pace, passing three very tall smokestacks that I imagine were at one time used as part of some type of refinery machinery, possibly phosphate. We have moved about 350 yards up this road and coming over a rise . . . I can see Marines already there ahead of me. And, as we draw closer to them, they are recognized as the forward echelon of good old Charlie Company. They cleaned out the ravine and are on the road taking it fairly easy and waiting for Captain Pope to come up and give them the dope for this evening.

The company is now situated in a bad spot should the enemy choose to drop in on us with tanks or even mortars. The picture is this: the coral road I have spoken of so much this afternoon runs almost parallel to the coast line on the southwestern side of the island and is bordered inland by a series of rough coral ridges rising almost 300 feet in some places, and running nearly to the end of the island. The position of the company at present puts the road on our left flank as we move north and west up the island. Across the road, L Company of the 3d

Battalion is tying in with us and the 3d Battalion lines extend to the beach, back to C Company. Our company front is in a northeasterly direction. The road on our left flank divides a low hill, giving the appearance of a definite pass between two cliffs. Company headquarters is just back of this pass and off to the right of the road in an area, which looks as though it had been recently evacuated. The platoons on the line extend from the right side of the road up the hill and on the side of the ridge facing the enemy. We in the CP can step out to the road and look several hundred yards into enemy territory. It is getting dark now and we are getting set for the night; barbed wire has come up and also ammunition and water. The gunnery sergeant has rejoined us and feels a great deal better. It has cooled off considerably.

Wait a minute. Something is going on up the hill to our right front.

Yes, indeed. The goddamned Japs are throwing mortar shells at us again and are knocking hell out of our men up there who are trying to find a place to dig in. Here come some of the men now, plunging down the side of the hill and onto the road, some bleeding profusely from nasty open jagged shrapnel wounds, some are being helped down by their buddies, unable to make it alone.

Jesus Christ! Here comes Gunny [Thomas H.] McHugh, Sergeants [Stanley P.] Rapacz, [Winston F.] Fontaine, and a flock of others, all bleeding like stuck hogs. They are all trying to talk and tell the story of what is going on up there on the hill. Privates First Class [James C.] Lockamy [Jr.], [Walter T.] Lee, and numerous others have come down off the hill wounded and assisting the wounded. Lockamy has both his knee caps blown off and is in great pain. The third platoon seems to be getting the worst of it, and here comes Platoon Sergeant [Frank] Misiak, staggering drunkenly towards the CP.

THRAAK ! THRAAAK!

★★★★★★

Good God, they're tossing them in on the command post now and we've all hit the deck trying to find something to get behind. Those that are wounded and lying on stretchers may be hit again. The stretcher bearers are taking the chance of getting cut in half but they are going out after their loads.

KA WHAM! KA WHAM!

Now it's grenades and two of the stretcher bearers are downed in their tracks. Lieutenant [Weldon] Longbotham has also been hit and has a very bewildered look upon his face. How badly he is hit we don't know yet. He may not be too badly off as he has recovered slightly from the shock of the blast. The mortars and grenades have stopped falling and the frantic cries for corpsmen are heard over the loud talking and general confusion in the CP.

Captain Pope is on the phone now and trying his best to get battalion on the other end. He is speaking now and I hear him saying "Jim." He must be talking to Captain Rogers, the operations officer. He is explaining the situation thoroughly to him, covering every detail. Now he is asking Rogers for some support by artillery or mortar fire to keep the Nipponese illegitimates in their holes long enough for us to at least clear out the wounded and get dug in for the night. We are suffering about three casualties per minute.[23]

The conversation is over now and the captain is conversing with Lieutenant Stanford of the Naval Observer Group and Lieutenant Hilliard, the forward observer from the 11th Marines. Both of these officers are going to get their radios in operation and call for fire from their respective organizations. Lieutenant Hilliard is going to ask for a battalion of artillery to open up as soon as he gets contact with them

---

[23] The USMC monograph by Maj Hough, quoting a letter from Maj Ray Davis, the battalion commander, states that at this point, although Charlie Company had been able to move 800 yards, it had become seriously overextended (Hough, 81). Davis maintains that everything possible was done to reinforce the success of C/1/1, and that "remnants of Companies A and B, Engineer and Pioneer units were committed to fill the gaps as darkness came," but there is no indication of this in 1stSgt Ainsworth's narrative. The pattern of an advance by C Company without adequate support on its flanks would be repeated on the following day and night.

and is able to give them the proper coordinates. Lieutenant Stanford is now calling on the USS *Mississippi* (BB-41) for support. The *Mississippi* is laying off shore and will start throwing in the big stuff as soon as the correct coordinates are given her. If that doesn't put a stop to the enemy mortar action, we may as well pack up our duds and catch the first train for Oshkosh.

Lieutenant Longbotham was hit in the foot and is hobbling off down the road to the aid station. It's getting much too dark to see now and the hostile barrage has lifted. The men are back on the hill in their positions, setting up defenses, digging emplacements where the ground permits, and stringing barbed wire as a further measure of security.

ZZZZZOP!

Down! Down for God's sake! Hit the deck!

It's a knee mortar shell and its nose is stuck down in the sand, it hasn't gone off yet but it may.

"Stand clear of the damn thing," yells the Captain, "it may go off."

We stood clear all right, and how! Whew! Man, oh man, if any one of the dozen men in the CP had a ball bat he could have taken one step and poled that one right out of the park. There it lays, fully exposed in the sand, only about four inches long and about as big around as one of those good old five-cent pickles you used to get at your neighborhood butcher shop. But mister, there's more misery and death in one of those insignificant looking green striped pellets than you can possibly conceive of. They're murder.[24]

Well I'm writing in the dark now and as I look closer at my memo pad, I can see that the last three lines are on the back of my hand so it's time to quit.[25]

---

[24]The Japanese Type 89 Heavy Grenade Discharger was known as a knee mortar because it was erroneously believed to be fired by being braced against the knee. It was lighter and fired from shorter range than a conventional mortar. Of the eight Medals of Honor awarded at Peleliu, six—five posthumously—were given to men who threw their bodies on grenades or artillery shells to save their fellow Marines.
[25] This is an indication of how the narrative was composed.

Taken in late October 1944, this photo graphically shows the effect naval gunfire support had on the Peleliu beachhead. The area is literally covered with shell craters. Note the antitank trench from left to right across the bottom of the photograph, and the plot of graves at far right center.
U.S. Navy USH 283519

18

★ ★ ★ ★ ★ ★
SEPTEMBER 1944

Today begins our fourth day of fighting on PELELIU during which time we have paid dearly in lives and blood for the meager holdings already conquered. It has been a desperate fight for every inch of ground taken. Since yesterday's attack, which started at 0800, through .02 and the advance on .03, this company alone has sustained 51 men wounded and evacuated, and one killed. Many of the wounded are in critical condition and their prognosis is poor.[26]

Immediately after dark last night, Jap mortars, hand grenades, and artillery began falling in on our lines again. Lieutenant Stanford got in radio contact with the battleship *Mississippi*, and after giving her coordinates of targets to be fired upon, he shut down his set and we waited for the first salvo. It wasn't long in coming and after about four salvos, Lieutenant Stanford contacted them and made the proper corrections in range and deflection and asking them to fire one salvo every 30 seconds all night long or [until] he gave orders to cease firing. He again shut down the radio and we sat back in the protection of an emplacement made of full cases of ammunition and awaited the sweet music from the nine big guns of that lovely lady, "Miss *Mississippi*."

All night long she kept up the barrage throwing in about three shells every half-a-minute and occasionally she would open up with

---

[26] Based on these figures, Charlie Company had sustained more than 22 percent casualties. As the company first sergeant, Ainsworth was responsible for keeping count of the company's effective strength. Losses had been heavy for the entire 1st Marines, with a total of 1,236 casualties at this point in the battle (Hough, 81). Col Lewis B. "Chesty" Puller nevertheless remained optimistic in his reports to division, confidently anticipating a breakthrough on the next day (Hough 81–82).

★★★★★★

all nine guns in a grand broadside salvo. The naval gunfire together with the artillery support from the 11th Marines definitely kept the Nips in their caves allowing us to relax a little. But when the firing from the artillery batteries would cease for the shortest period—WHAM WHAM WHAM!—in would come the mortars again.

Lieutenant Hilliard called the battery and asked them why they did not keep firing. The answer came back over the ether, "Are you sure you have a target to shoot at? You know we're using up a hell of a lot of ammunition."

Geez, ain't it a crying shame. What a moxie these guys have asking us if we have a target to shoot at. I don't know, maybe those cannoneers are paying for the stuff they sent our way. . . . If we wanted to be nasty about it, we could truthfully tell them that up to now the *Mississippi* has been getting the hits and that the battery that is supposed to be supporting us is an also-ran. But we are courteous about it and the lieutenant tells them in a very assuring manner that they're "right on target and to keep firing." A little smoke blowing now and then will accomplish much and as long as they keep firing, the Nips will keep down in their holes and give the mortars a rest. God knows they need it. They sure have in plenty of overtime.[27]

To add to the night's discomfort, the area where we are was kept illuminated very brightly all night by both friendly and hostile flares. "Lady Godiva" no doubt felt a bit undressed in her rather risqué ride from Boston or wherever it was to Lexington, passing out the dope on the advancing British, but under those flares on PELELIU we felt like nudes at a Sid Grauman world premier—AND HOW![28]

---

[27] A gap between the flanks of the 1st and 2nd Battalions had opened after dark, but "any overwhelming counterattack which might have made the situation something worse than precarious was effectively interdicted by concentrations of well-placed artillery and naval gunfire on the approaches" (Hough, 81)

[28] Ainsworth's confusion of Lady Godiva with Paul Revere is probably intended as a joke. In 1938, a celebrated show at Sid Grauman's Chinese Theater in Hollywood had featured two nude women standing motionless under spotlights on each side of the stage, strategically posed, while police watched to make sure they stayed absolutely still throughout the entire performance.

The time is now 0700 and it has been quiet for the past couple of hours. We expect to be relieved sometime today to return to the blockhouse area for a few hours rest and a hot meal. We can certainly use both.

0719 and some of our own tanks are down in front of our line and shooting up a storm with machine guns. I don't know what the score is. They are our tanks alright and have shot hell out of some of our own men, having mistaken them for Japs. Captain Pope is trying to get in touch with the tank commanders by a tank radio which is setting alongside of our CP. He is having a devil of a time, still no contact whatsoever.

Private First Class Jurgens has stood up in front of the oncoming tanks and is waving his arms wildly and trying to make himself heard

by the occupants of the tanks that they are Marines not Nips. Down he goes under a hail of bullets and the tanks continue to fire. Captain Pope has now made contact with the tank commanders and they are responding to his pleas to "for God's sake stop shooting my men!"[29]

It's quiet again now and we are collecting our wounded from this last costly case of mistaken identity. There aren't a hell of a lot of us left in the company any more, but we intend to carry on the fight to the last man if necessary. There are no quitters in this outfit. Any man that is lost to us is lost by enemy action, not by fright. These men don't scare worth a damn, and though many have gone down, they're by no means counted out.[30]

I stood by one of my kids who was badly wounded and listened to him talking to his buddy who was helping the corpsman administer first aid with all the tenderness of a woman. The kid hated to leave, but when the litter bearers picked up his stretcher and started to move away, he sat upright and grabbed his buddy's hand, and with tears of

---

[29] This friendly fire incident is not mentioned in any of the histories of Peleliu, including Hough's detailed official monograph. The forward lines were often fluid: "When company commanders were asked for the front line, they were apt to give points where the company commander knew or thought he knew he had some men" (Hough, 83).

[30] This could be dismissed as bravado—if the men of Charlie Company had not indeed fought virtually to the last man.

The area just off the Peleliu beachhead was Company C's resting place on 18 September. Rest and relaxation had to be found in a scene like this, with the added impact of the remains of the dead and the stench of their decay.
Headquarters U.S. Marine Corps 95247

anger running down his cheeks he sobbed, "Kick hell out of those rotten yellow sons-a-bitches, cobber, I'll be back in a couple of days."[31] Exhibiting the fight that still burned within him, he departed. He did not return nor do we expect him back.

The time is now 0800 and here comes our relief up the road in column of twos. As soon as Captain Pope takes the K Company CO around, showing him our lines, flanks, and what few vantage points we command, K Company will take up our positions and we will revert to regimental reserve. For how long we have no idea, but the thoughts uppermost in our minds at present are sponge baths, sleep, and some hot food and perhaps some real coffee.[32]

It is 0830 and we are in reserve at last. It's a bad area to have to live in, due to the stench of the bloated, rotting corpses scattered every few yards over the coral and torn up vegetation. I imagine that every fly in the western Carolines is in on this picnic, the air is thick with them. The burial parties have already started the unpleasant, but highly essential task of consigning the dead to their graves. "The Imperial Nipponese Burial Service" ain't what it could be, but that's O.K. We can stand the smell. Let 'em rot.

Some of the men are already taking what is known in the Marine

---

[31] *Cobber* is Australian usage for "friend." The 1st Marine Division had picked up Australian slang during its period of recuperation in Melbourne after Guadalcanal.
[32] The remnants of Capt George Hunt's company, decimated in the battle on the Point, were now being sent in to replace Charlie Company on the front lines.

★★★★★

Corps as a whore's bath, using their helmet for water and half a towel to wash with, the other half for drying. Others too tired to wash just yet are clearing a space on the deck where they can flake out until time to eat. Still others are fast asleep, using their canteens or shoes for pillows.

Sergeant Charlie Monarch and I took a walk about noon—a stroll through the area where our battle of the night of the 16th and 17th had taken place—counting 112 "good" Japs and many dead Marines, the Japs total being nearly five times higher than ours.

There sticks in my mind an incident, which at the time amused both Charlie and me very much. We were standing over the carcass of a huge Jap marine whose body was almost completely decomposed, the last bit of flesh having fallen off his face as we had walked up, jarring the ground. Looking at the blackened skull we stood amazed, gaping at a small fortune. This Nip had two full sets of solid gold teeth, uppers and lowers alike, the biggest teeth I have ever seen.

Charlie and I looked at each other, then back at the teeth, then back at each other down and up until we both started feeling like drunks at a tennis match. All of a sudden a voice from behind shattered the silence of the eerie scene with a loud "Nice teeth, ain't they?"

Rather startled we spun around, looking at a tall skinny kid with a foolish grin on his face and a big pair of pliers in his left hand.

"Just a minute, Butch," says Charlie, "You can't do that, you know the orders!"

"You're damned right," I told the goof, "International law, the Geneva conference, remember?"

The goof's eyes narrowed to mere slits. "You guys must be nuts. Better get out of the sun before you really get punchy."

He turned away, picked up a big reel of phone wire, hoisted it onto his shoulders, and with a last glance over his shoulder at us, walked away shaking his head. Charlie and I watched him for a while, looked and each other again and back at the wireman.

"Just a minute, Top," said Monarch, "Let's not go into that head-shaking deal again. We'll get punchy sure as hell. In fact I think there is something in what that guy said. I think . . ."

"Well quit thinking," I told him, "and let's get out of this place." We returned to the company area. The Nip kept his teeth.[33]

The remainder of the day was spent in preparing shelters and places to sleep tonight, getting cleaned up as much as possible, and waiting for "chow call." We were called to chow at 1700. The battalion galley is set up near the blockhouse that is now being used as the battalion aid station and command post. Stack upon stack of clover leafs of mortar ammunition surround the galley area, and Marines are sitting all over the ammunition, on the ground, and anywhere else where there is room to sit down and enjoy a good hot meal with "real coffee." Supper consisted of corn, peas, sausage, boned chicken, peanut butter, crackers, and coffee.

No one who wasn't there can possibly conceive of how good that hot meal tasted to the men on this night. It took more than an hour to feed all the men in the battalion who were in reserve, plus the attached units, and at 1830 I passed the word that in ten minutes the smoking lamp would be out for the night, so light your last one now.

It is dark now and the men are all in their foxholes and under ponchos, which will partially shelter them from the rains that are due to catch us anytime now. We have excellent weather and no rain at all. Perhaps it would be better if we had a few showers during the day. It might keep the heat exhaustion down some. I find it too dark to write more tonight, so until morning I'll say, so long for today.

---

[33] That Ainsworth could characterize this as an "amusing" incident, and that he and his fellow senior NCO could be tempted to mutilate the corpse, speaks volumes for the state of mind of the men of the 1st Marines.

The Marines of Company C used this route across the swamp for their first assault against Hill 100, prominent in the background, on 19 September.
U.S. Marine Corps

19

★ ★ ★ ★ ★ ★ ★
SEPTEMBER 1944

It is now 0545 and all hands are awake and on the lookout for any snipers that might have infiltrated our lines during the night. [We] are waiting for it to get light enough for them to get a pot shot at us. As it continues to get lighter, we relax our vigil after very carefully giving all the trees, brush, and possible places of concealment a close scrutiny. For once our findings were negative.

At about 2100 last night, a sniper got within range of the blockhouse and hurled a grenade in an attempt to inflict [further harm on] casualties already on stretchers in the aid station awaiting evacuation. His attempt was unsuccessful in its original purpose, but in falling short of his intended target, [the grenade] dropped into a shell hole in which there were a number of men and wounded six of them. Several hours later the same sniper tried to repeat his act of infamy but his plans were upset by an alert Browning automatic rifleman who had been posted at one corner of the blockhouse as a guard against a recurrence of the earlier attack.

Daylight this morning revealed the Jap quite dead with a small hole (about the size of a shovel handle) cleanly through his head, allowing his brains to leak out both sides, giving him the appearance of wearing horns. The Nip was without shoes which no doubt enabled him to get as close as he did without being detected by men in the vicinity.

The time is now 0615 and the men have started small fires over

★★★★★

which they are brewing coffee and heating up the C rations that have just been issued. Perhaps the galley force will come through with some of the old-fashioned coffee later on.

It is 0705, and we have received orders to relieve Baker Company. We will attack at 0845. Baker Company yesterday attacked a ridge known as Hill 154, stormed and captured it only to be thrown off a few hours later under withering automatic weapons fire and numerically superior enemy forces. Baker Company has suffered a heavy toll of casualties, necessitating their immediate relief. The same ridge is the one Charlie Company is going to attack at 15 minutes to nine this morning.[34]

It is now 0743 and the company is in a column stretching some distance down the road in front of the blockhouse and waiting on Captain Pope, who is at present in a huddle with Majors [Ray] Davis, Stevenson, and Captain [James] Rogers, the battalion operations officer. The huddle has finally broken up, a few good lucks are wished. Captain Pope is on his way over to me now and in just a couple of seconds I'll have the picture. Here it is: we will attack, battalions abreast, 2d Battalion on the left, 1st Battalion on the right, at exactly 0845.[35]

All men synchronize watches. In 35 seconds it will be exactly 0810.

Twenty seconds.

Ten seconds.

Stand by . . .

Mark!

Charlie Company—stand by to move out.

Captain Pope is moving up to the head of the column and in just a

---

[34] Company B's progress had been halted by the complex ridge system known as the Five Sisters. The last pocket of resistance there would be overcome only months later, in November, after prolonged artillery preparation by the Army's 81st Division.

[35] This was in accordance with the order of the day from the commander of the 1st Marine Division, MajGen Rupertus: "All infantry units will resume the attack with maximum effort in all sectors at 0830 hrs on September 19." He had little sense of the situation faced by the 1st Marines. One battalion commander wrote later, "There was no such thing as a continuous attacking line. Elements of the same company, even platoons, were attacking in every direction of the compass, with large gaps in between" (Hough, 84).

jiffy we'll be underway to the point we start the attack from. The column has turned off the road leading to the blockhouse and are on a rough, winding road that leads up to the front lines. [We are] passing through the shop area and part of a barracks and blockhouse area that probably was the headquarters of the Jap air force stationed here. Several hundred yards to our right front are several airplane hangars or, perhaps I should say, what is left of airplane hangars, and through the gap between [them] are seen rows of Nip planes, destroyed on the ground.

We are swinging to the northeast now, and the road has straightened out before us but is up-grade, and only those at the head of the column can see the ridge we are going to attack. As the tail end of the column reaches the high point in the road, I can see not only the ridge in question, but three additional ones all equally high and steep, both to the left and right and, incidentally, still in enemy hands.

There is very little wonder in any of our minds that Baker Company lost this ridge. In fact I don't see how they captured it to begin with. They must have been completely outflanked on both sides and receiving plunging fire from higher ground beyond the nose of the ridge.[36]

We are moving off the road now and going into attack formation, tying in with the second battalion on our left. We have several hundred yards in front to cover and some distance ahead of us [is] a torn-up Japanese bivouac area through which the company must pass in a skirmish line. This area is studded with concrete bunkers, pillboxes, and cement pillars, which were at one time the foundation of many corrugated iron buildings. Providing that there are not snipers behind all these obstacles, they will afford excellent cover for the men in our advance.

---

[36] This was Ainsworth's first glimpse of the "incredible complex of upended peaks and palisades, which was to gain evil fame under the name of the Five Sisters" (Hough, 83).

An F4U Corsair pulls up after delivering its payload of napalm on embedded Japanese defenders in the hills of Umurbrogol Mountain.
Headquarters U.S. Marine Corps 07977

★★★★★★

The time is now 0839, and in six minutes we jump off. Captain Pope is quite distant from me now, and although I cannot hear his voice, I can see him motioning with his arms to his flanks, bringing them up on the line as a captain of a football team lines his forward wall up for the kick-off. My skipper is a master in the field, and the men have every confidence in him and he in them.

0843, two minutes to go, and I am moving my CP directly in behind the company, exactly between our flanks, ready to occupy a pre-arranged position in the bivouac area, get them under cover, establish communications with the rear (if possible), and await further orders from the company commander as soon as he gets situated up front.

Thirty seconds to go and the men up and down the lines are checking their watches, there is some sniper fire from the swamp and ridges up forward and occasionally a mortar shell or an 88mm explodes near the lines, but so far I haven't heard the call for corpsmen. The sun is really beating down today and it will get hotter up to noon; I hope the guys conserve their water, I have a feeling they're going to need it before very long.

Here we go, it's 0845 on the head and the lines are moving forward fast. There is little firing going on at present. They are moving in through the bivouac area now and dodging from pillar to pillar, but always in a forward movement, crouching for a second, then up and sprinting to the next place of protection.

A Nambu machine gun has opened up, and some of the men on the extreme left of our company have gone down, [or] it may be men on the right flank of the second battalion. I can't tell from here.

Company headquarters is up and on the move, making for the bivouac area in groups of twos and threes, also taking advantage of the cover as they advance. The forward elements are entering the edge of the mangrove swamps now and the firing has become deafening. All automatic weapons are going full blast from both sides. Bullets are whining over our heads, banging into the concrete pillars the men are behind, and throwing cement all over the place. The [men] are starting to holler for corpsmen and some stretchers now. The demands for stretchers and corpsmen are increasing by the second. All my corpsmen are forward in the lines now, and I've had to use every available man in headquarters to send in as stretcher bearers.

[Field Musician First Class Roscoe L.] Wagner[37] is the only man left here with me, and I'm going to send him on a run to find the captain just as soon as the first man returns from the front lines. Our radio can't contact the 1st Battalion directly, and all calls have to be relayed through Fox Company of the 2d Battalion.[38] The set is jammed with messages already and there is no telling when the operator will have a chance to send a message to Major Stevenson for me. Some of the men are coming out of the swamp carrying wounded and I'm dispatching Wagner to locate Captain Pope to bring me the situation and any orders he may have for me.[39]

The time, 0930, and here comes a runner from the swamps covered with mud and slime. He has a message for me to send to White 6 requesting immediate tank support. The entire line is pinned down by heavy– and light–machine gun fire, and our casualties are increasing. The runner tells me that the company on our left, K Company, 2d Battalion, is really getting the hell kicked out of them by the enemy

---

[37] Wagner must have been the company bugler in other times.

[38] In this attack, "Companies F and G had to be combined with a squad from the War Dog Platoon to make up a single skeleton company" (Hough, 84). The War Dog Platoon typically consisted of one officer, 65 men, and 36 dogs (18 scout and 18 messenger). A squad was composed of 6 scout dogs and handlers, 6 messenger dogs and 12 handlers, and a noncommissioned officer in charge.

[39] With Wagner's departure, the company headquarters consisted solely of 1stSgt Ainsworth. Everyone else had gone forward. Ainsworth had to stay behind because he was responsible for maintaining contact between his former commanding officer, Maj Nikolai Stevenson at battalion, and the front lines. Phone lines had obviously not been laid, and thus the only communication was with unreliable short-range radios.

machine guns and mortars. The mortars are bursting in on the tops of the trees and sending down a regular umbrella of shrapnel. I have sent this same runner to give the message of Captain Pope to White 6.

As the sun climbs in the sky the heat becomes more intense. Most of the men who went into the swamp to bring out the wounded have come out now and are getting their breath, leaning forward with the hands on their knees. I hope to God that Wagner makes it O.K. and comes back with news that we haven't been too badly hit. He's been gone damn near an hour now and no word from the skipper. I have managed to contact Major Stevenson and have asked for at least 15 stretchers and double the number of stretcher bear-ers, the message was sent "urgent."

The rugged terrain of Peleliu provides an almost surreal environment for a column of Marines as it moves up to the front lines. Natural caves and heavily fortified bunkers and pillboxes dotted the hellish landscape.
Headquarters U.S. Marine Corps 96764

1140, and here comes Wagner. I thought he must have been hit and couldn't get through to the captain or had gotten it on his way back. He is so completely exhausted he can't even talk. I've lighted a cigarette and put it between his lips, and am trying to get him a drink of water from my canteen. He has quieted down a bit, and is trying to give me the picture. Here it is: our entire line is pinned down, unable to advance a yard. There are two concrete pillboxes situated on the very tip of two prominent peninsulas, which extend out into the swamps, they are on high ground and have the whole line in a murderous crossfire. Together with the mortar fire and artillery they have just recently turned against us, we are in a very bad spot. Wagner started shaking violently and I have ordered him to the rear, giving him one more message to give to Major Stevenson when he gets back to battalion. The message contains the situation as it is at present.

Captain Pope has ordered me to stay in my present position for the time being. There are a few snipers shooting at us from the swamps on our right, and anyone who sticks their head up to have a "look see" is a plain chump.

It is now 1150, and I have gotten a message to send to Captain Pope, from White 6, it reads "Tanks on the way as requested. Signed: CO, LT.21."[40] Maybe the tanks can stop the slaughter that is going on in the swamps or at least neutralize the two gun positions. Our artillery and mortars have opened up, but the effectiveness is not yet determined.

It is 1202 now and another message from "White 6" has come through, on its way to Captain Pope. It reads, "Do not withdraw, hold what you've got."[41] O.K., so we hold what we've got, but what in hell have we got to hold? A handful of swamps perhaps, nothing more.

1234 and the tanks are on the way up the road to try and knock out the main points of resistance in and around the swamp. They are throwing everything they have at the two pillboxes that house those two deadly machine guns. Our mortars are reaching up the nose of the ridge in an effort to blast out the enemy artillery and mortar positions. Our men are still in the swamp and haven't moved up an inch in the last two

---

[40] LtCol Russell E. Honsowetz, CO of the 2d Battalion, 1st Marines. Charlie Company had been attached to the 2d Battalion for this operation, hence the order from Honsowetz rather than from Majors Davis or Stevenson at 1/1. Honsowetz was under heavy pressure from Col Puller, who had told him to take the ridge by nightfall at any cost.

[41] Pope would not be granted permission to withdraw for another three and a half hours.

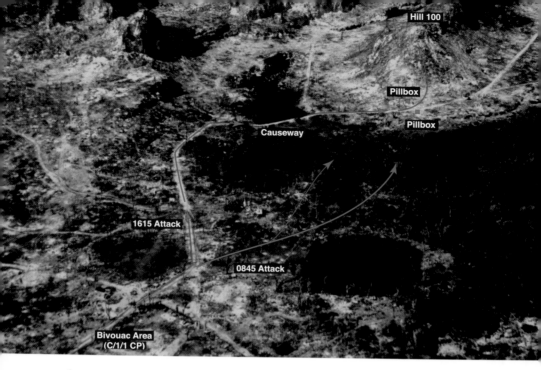

Hill 100

Pillbox

Pillbox

Causeway

1615 Attack

0845 Attack

Bivouac Area
(C/1/1 CP)

hours. Our two very capable platoon leaders, Lieutenants Shaffner and Burke, are doing a fine job in the holding action but it looks hopeless.

The sun is becoming unbearable and many men have been evacuated to the rear, passed completely out from heat exhaustion. I can't help but think that a withdrawal will be ordered before long, I don't see what else they can do. We're getting absolutely no place through the swamps and the casualties are rising in count by the minute. However, it's not my business to question strategy. It's possible that the man in charge has something up his sleeve besides his arm. I hope it's an order to pull back and reorganize. There must be another way to take the ridge.[42]

The time is now 1530 and the order to withdraw has finally come

---

[42] The synopsis of these events in the 1950 USMC monograph is somewhat misleading: "Company C approached through the swamp and reached the road at the base of the hill, where two strong pillboxes were discovered. The men were in the process of assaulting these when they were suddenly pinned down by machine gun fire at a range of about 50 yards from a small pool on their right. Unable to get at these assailants, the captain obtained permission to withdraw the way he had come, pass to the left of the main lagoon, and attack up the road with the support of tanks" (Hough, 84). But it is clear from Ainsworth's narrative that Pope's initial request to be allowed to withdraw was rejected. Instead, he was told to hold on at all costs, and he and his men held their positions for another three hours at least, suffering casualties to no purpose. By the time he finally received permission to "withdraw the way he had come," Charlie Company had been pinned down in the swamp under heavy fire for most of the day.

The routes of Company C's two assaults of 19 September on Hill 100 are
depicted on a battlefield photograph.
U.S. Marine Corps

through. The men are pulling back and here comes the skipper. He looks worn out. So do the rest of the guys. Slimy black mud all over them, weapons covered with it, men without weapons, men with weapons that have ceased to function, with entire stocks shattered by machine gun and mortar fire.

The skipper started this way but stopped and took off for the 2d Battalion command post. I can see him conversing with White 6. Now he's coming back this way and seems to be in a big hurry. I'll get the dope in a few minutes.

The men are all out of the swamps now and are in platoon groups talking it over and getting what rest they can in case we have to go back in the attack this afternoon. It's getting late and if we are going to take the ridge today, they better get hot. Platoons are in the process of reorganizing and I'm going to ask for an exact count of effectives. Ammunition is being distributed and the men are trying their best to clean up their mud-caked weapons and put them in working order again. D rations are being passed out to all the men wanting them and all canteens are being filled.

Here comes Capt Pope!

He starts to talk, "O.K. Top, here's the picture. White 6 is throwing us back in the attack again in just 30 minutes. We will attack the ridge, from a different angle this time, using dry ground and skirting the swamps."

"Thirty minutes! Jesus Christ skipper, these guys need a rest!"

"I know, Top, but there's not a thing in the world I can do about it. The orders from White 6 are Charlie Company will attack and capture that ridge before dark. You will attack at 1615. We will have three tanks in support as we move in. The first and second platoons will deploy to the left and right of the road. Keep company headquarters in close to

★★★★★★

the assault platoons. Do not lose contact whatever you do. Have Monarch's assault team follow directly behind the reserve machine guns. We're going to need him as soon as we get over that causeway. He'll have plenty of work to do. How many men have we available for the attack?"

"Ninety-four enlisted, four officers. There are 12 or 13 men who will probably fold up before we get to the causeway. The heat has them in a bad way right now."

"O.K., tell the worst ones to remain behind, the others can go as they feel able."

It's 1605, and we are again in a skirmish line extended across the road and getting set. None of the heat cases are staying behind, they refuse. What a company this is!

Planes are working over the ridge in a big way now. Dive bombing, strafing, and firing their rockets. All the artillery on the island has opened up. At least it sounds that way. We're ready to go now. It's 1612 and the tanks are already moving up the road and on both flanks.

WE'RE OFF!

It's too noisy now to give oral commands and the use of hand and arm signals is being employed. So far so good. There are Jap snipers working on our left flank along with a light machine gun. One of the tanks is changing its course to get into position and knock out the opposition on that flank. He's moving right in on them.

Two Japs came up out of spider traps that were in line with our charging Shermans and are attempting to climb up on the back of the tank. The pistol port opens, and a .45 Colt automatic starts popping at the two Nips. The guy in the tank nailed them both. The pistol port closes, the turret swings around to the front, and the big 75mm starts blasting at the machine gun nest.[43]

---

[43] From the USMC monograph: "The first tank to attempt the causeway slipped over to one side and became immobilized. A second tank, in an attempt to extricate it, slipped off the other side, thus blocking the narrow approach to further supporting arms" (Hough, 85).

I'm watching this action from a shell crater about 50 yards from the left of the causeway, the assault team is deployed to my right. Charlie Monarch is walking upright following close behind the machine gun squads in reserve. He is a picture of calm and unconcern, with his pack of high explosives slung over his arm. He has just beckoned to some of his men to come up and help him with making up a charge.

Earlier today Monarch was talking to me and mentioned the fact that the only pair of shoes he has to his name are on his feet and shot to hell. He asked me what size I wore. I told him, "eight-and-one-half double-E." Giving my gunboats the once over, he remarked, "Damn good shape, too," and walked away. Hmm—I wonder what he was thinking?[44]

The entire line is nearing the point where the causeway crosses from the right side of the road, over the swamp, and connects with the

---

[44] Sgt Charles Monarch must have been killed soon after this during the assault on Hill 100. If Ainsworth had edited his notes later, this joke about his friend eyeing his boots would have been excised after the fact. It is clear that Monarch had by then earned his posthumous Navy Cross many times over.

★★★★★★

base of the ridge. The time is 1643, and we're breaking through the resistance and getting up on the causeway at several different places. The two assault platoons are now tearing wildly across the coral and log causeway and many have already reached the bottom of the hill.[45] The tankers are pounding the large concrete artillery emplacements with their 75s and are moving across the causeway with the men.[46] Some of our machine guns have set up at the junction of the road and causeway and are building up a base of fire, covering the advance of our riflemen as they start the tough climb up the steep sides of the ridge.

[45] "Company C crossed it in squad rushes, paused momentarily at the foot of the hill, then assaulted it with only mortar and machine gun support" (Hough, 85).
[46] The two Shermans subsequently became immobilized on either side of the causeway (Hough, 85.)

Marines, most likely of the 7th Marines, climb Hill 100 later in the battle. This provides a graphic sense of what Company C faced as they fought their way up the hill.
U.S. Marine Corps

This ridge has been under continuous air, artillery, and naval bombardment since before D-day, and the pulverized coral rock covers the sides of the ridge making it difficult to gain headway as you climb. Every step taken nets only inches of gain. Charlie Company is now swarming over the face of the ridge like so many Moros running amok.[47] They are shouting and hollering as they go up the steep slope, stopping now and again to fire at a target in one of the many holes in the hillside. The Japs are pulling out now and moving back further from the very nose of the ridge. The Marines are in hot pursuit.

I'm over the causeway with company headquarters now and moving in behind the Japanese 88mm position. Private First Class [Donald P.] Christner[48] is with me and we decide to throw a few grenades into the partly demolished emplacement just as a measure of caution before going further around the ridge. It's possible there may be a sniper in there waiting a chance to start shooting us in the back as we pass by.

WHAM. WHAM. WHAM. There go our grenades and the pillbox is secured. There is a dead Nip laying just outside the back door, with no top to his head. His rifle is in his mouth, and the big toe on his left foot is caught in his trigger guard. More of these jokers should follow this guy's idea. The war would be over a helluva a lot sooner.

Two of our men are now tackling an enemy machine gun by themselves. They are trying to scale the side of the hill, which is nearly straight up and down. Other men in the company and one tank is supporting their daring attack. It looks as if they might make the grade. They are about 15 feet apart and climbing steadily. I can't make out just who it is because their backs are towards me.

BAM! BAM!

Good God, a terrific explosion has gone off right between the two of them and they are lost to sight by the smoke and dusk. I don't see

---

[47] The reference to the Moros of Mindanao is a curious bit of Marine lore, handed down by the Old Breed to which 1stSgt Ainsworth belonged.
[48] PFC Christner was wounded the following day, and he died on 21 September.

how either one of them can have missed being hit. The smoke is clearing up a bit now, and there is something down the side of the hill tumbling and rolling. It's one of the two men. The other man is still high up on the side of the ridge, laying face down, and missing a leg.

What men of the company have not yet crossed the causeway are doing so now. The first men are nearly on the summit of the ridge. Captain Pope is on the very top with Sergeant McAlarnis and a host of others.[49] More men are gaining the top and the Nips are in disorderly retreat.

1703, we have definitely taken the ridge and are mopping up stragglers. The immediate problem at hand now is to get dug in and get set for an inevitable counterattack. Captain Pope has a radio and its operator up on top of the hill with him. I also have a radioman and the same type set the skipper has, but the captain cannot contact White 6 with his set and I can, therefore all messages to CO LT. 21 must be relayed through me. My CP is about halfway up the side of the hill on the right, in what was a Jap field piece and machine gun position just until an hour ago when the attack started.

Our line now extends from the top of the ridge, down the right side, pulling slightly back as it straggles down the hill to where my CP is located. One platoon of the First Reconnaissance Company is coming up to tie in with my company's right flank and they comprise the rest of the line down to the bottom of the hill and just over the road. On their

---

[49] Sgt James P. McAlarnis was awarded the Navy Cross. The citation reads in part: "With his platoon assigned the mission of seizing the strongly defended summit of Hill 100, a coral nose studded with caves and concrete emplacements, Platoon Sergeant McAlarnis boldly led elements of his unit through intense hostile fire to the top of the hill and then assisted his Platoon Leader in deploying his men despite fire from a fieldpiece on an adjoining ridge. On several occasions, he engaged the enemy in fierce hand-to-hand combat, and, when his Leader was wounded and pinned to the ground by a bayonet in the hand of a Japanese, boldly rushed to his comrade's aid. Throwing himself upon the enemy, he beat him into submission and hurled him over a cliff. When his platoon's position became untenable the following morning, Platoon Sergeant McAlarnis remained until the last man had withdrawn." His platoon leader was 1stLt Francis T. Burke, who also received the Navy Cross. This instance of hand-to-hand combat is recounted below by Ainsworth, in vivid, though somewhat different terms.

right is L Company, 3d Battalion, but their lines pull back so far on their extreme right that they are useless as flank protection, and could almost be termed as a secondary line. "Maybe they're not so dumb after all."

It is 1800 and Captain Pope has sent word to White 6 that "we are on the hill, situation precarious. Cover our flanks. Send 37s to road on right."[50]

Here is another message for me to relay to the officer in charge of L Company: "To the company commander down below. For Christ's sake come up and cover our right. Get 37s to cover the road. Get tanks and call for artillery fire to our front. Have no communications. Signed: Captain Pope, C-1-1."[51]

In addition to company headquarters, in my CP there are the lieutenant in charge of the Recon Company platoon, his radioman, several corpsmen, more Recon Company personnel, some of which I have

---

[50] The reference is to the M3A1 37mm antitank gun.

[51] This plea for support went unanswered. Somewhat defensively, the 1950 monograph by Maj Hough suggests that it had not been the intention of the 2/1 commander, LtCol Honsowetz, to send the company against the ridge without adequate support on its flanks (Hough, 86). In his words, "Captain Pope had already carried the summit" before the second platoon of the Reconnaissance Company could get into position. Whatever Honsowetz's intentions may have been, in the event another platoon did not make much difference to C/1/1.

already taken advantage of and am using as perimeter defense for the CP. In addition to my own men, Lieutenants [Richard V.] Schall and Peck are on the outer rim of the niche and are establishing themselves as a mortar observation post.

We are in need of barbed wire and grenades along with small arms ammunition and plenty of men. I have sent word to the rear requesting these items. The answer is, "No men available, no 37s available, and no

Leathernecks in the left foreground watch as a flamethrower-equipped amphibious tractor spews a jet of flame into a Japanese-occupied cave.
National Archives and Records Administration 80-G-272912

tanks can get over the causeway due to one that is already out of action and cannot be moved out tonight."

Geez, that's fine. We take the goddamned ridge, and now we can't get anything we need to hold it. I am thinking "unkind thoughts" about the guy that recruited me in this outfit, because I'm not sure right now that it's on the level. Here we are, about 50 men left in the company since the attack, tied in with an outfit I've never heard of before, and being kept safe from Tojo's yellow hordes by a nondescript lash-up on our extreme "right rear."[52]

I dunno, maybe I don't have an elaborate enough imagination, but the way I look at things right now, puts everything in the "clam bake class." We have just enough concertinas to stretch from the top of the hill to a point halfway between my CP and the road below. At the other end of the wire is one machine gun, manned by a crew from the Recon Company, and on the right is another gun being manned by the same outfit. I have no idea what the defense is like beyond that. It's getting too dark to see anything at all.

Our defense for tonight is so flimsy it's pathetic, but there isn't a thing we can do about it. I just hope to hell those grenades get up here before it gets totally black. Private First Class [Dennis] De Hart has nearly had his right hand blow off by a Nip grenade and is standing on the side of the hill gazing bewilderedly at the mangled mass of flesh and bone dangling from the wrist while the corpsman is making his way over to him. Private First Class [William M.] Hallowell,[53] the radio operator with the captain, has been wounded in the eyes and is coming down from the top of the ridge being led by one of his buddies. Private First Class [Ralph] Leccaditto has also been hit and is being hurried to the rear before it gets pitch dark.

1900 and it is completely dark, not a trace of light left anywhere in

---

[52] The reference is to the Reconnaissance Company and to L/3/5.
[53] Hallowell had been attached to C/1/1 from the headquarters company, 1/1.

19 September | **63**

★★★★★★

the sky. Some shooting is going on at the bottom of the hill. A machine gun opens up with about a five-second burst and cuts off abruptly. They are calling for corpsmen, and hollering at the same time, "Japs inside the lines." This is the Recon Company and L Company sector. I thought so!

The corpsmen have reached the bottom of the hill and are attending whoever is wounded. It's quiet now, and a corpsman is coming back up to my position. Who is hit this time I asked him?

His reply startled me, "First Lieutenant Shaffner, (dead!)," he replied.

"Shaffner? Dead? What happened?"

Six Japs were within our lines and came jogging down the road toward their own lines, figuring that possibly with good luck they could pass as Marines. A gun crew of the Recon Company was busy getting ready to run a loaded belt through the machine gun when they heard the commotion on the road. They were talking with raised voices, and the man with the machine gun belt in his hands challenged them. They all stopped and crouched down on the road.

The ammunition carrier moved over closer to see who was there, and upon discovering they were Japs, belted the foremost one in the face with the heavily loaded belt of ammunition. The second Jap raised his weapon and fired, missing the Marine who had cooled off his cobber,[54] the bullet striking Lieutenant Shaffner in the chin and emerging from the back of his head. The machine gun got into action finally and got two of the Nips, but the other four escaped to their lines probably unharmed.

The loss of Lieutenant Shaffner is going to be felt by all the command. He was an ideal platoon leader, liked and respected by everyone. His outstanding performance of duty in this operation will be long

---

[54] This phrase presumably means hit his friend.

remembered by all those who have served with him. He did a superb job. He was a Marine's Marine.[55]

The mortars are now starting to throw up some illumination flares, which are falling short and exposing us to the enemy. Lieutenant Peck has called the battery and ordered them to put on the maximum range. If we are on this hill in the morning it'll be a surprise to a lot of people, including White 6. If we had three more machine guns, six or seven cases of grenades, and had time to install more concertinas and trip wires to hold us over until daybreak, we might be able to hold what we've got and possibly advance to the slightly higher ground where the Nips are holed up for tonight. As long as they control the high ground, they can roll grenades right into our laps all night long, and by morning we won't have anything left to fight with but our hands, but hand-to-hand fighting looks good in the newspapers back in the States, so if it comes to that, O.K.![56]

It is too dark to continue my notes so until tomorrow we're keeping our legs crossed and hoping for the best. The time is now 1952.

---

[55] The citation for the Navy Cross awarded posthumously to 1stLt Shaffner reads in part: "for extraordinary heroism while attached to the First Battalion, First Marines, First Marine Division, in action on Peleliu Island in the Palau Group, on 1 October 1944. Leading his tank-supported platoon against a steep coral ridge studded with caves and concrete machine-gun emplacements, First Lieutenant Shaffner pushed relentlessly forward despite terrific enemy mortar, machine-gun and antitank fire, which inflicted heavy casualties on his unit. Held up at a narrow causeway by the failure of communication with his armored vehicles, he climbed to a dangerous prominent vantage point on the turret of the leading tank, quickly organizing the fire of both vehicles and infantry, and, when his tanks still were unable to cross the fire-swept passage, placed himself at the head of the platoon and fearlessly led his men in a daring sweep through the devastating rain of fire and on to the objective. Repeatedly exposing himself to the enemy's unceasing barrage, he disposed his men for defense of the ridge, then organized and led a detail back across the causeway to bring up urgently needed ammunition. Mortally wounded while boldly carrying supplies to the most forward elements of his unit, First Lieutenant Shaffner had successfully fulfilled an extremely vital and hazardous mission and, by his determined aggressiveness, indomitable fighting spirit, and great personal valor in the face of terrific opposition, had contributed essentially to the ultimate conquest of the important Japanese stronghold." The date given in the citation is obviously incorrect.
[56] Unsupported, and running out of ammunition, Charlie Company was indeed reduced to hand-to-hand combat during the night, as the Japanese continued to attack from the high ground beyond Hill 100.

This is where it all began for Company C—White Beach 1. After six days of combat, what was left of the company was pulled out of the fight for a much needed respite. But even at that, on 22 September the company "exchanged grenades" with the enemy throughout the night.
Headquarters U.S. Marine Corps 95353

20

★★★★★★★
SEPTEMBER 1944

The time is now 0643. I'm resting alongside of Lieutenant Burke, Platoon Sergeant McAlarnis, and about seven of the men from the first platoon. We are no longer on the ridge. We were driven off at 0530 this morning. The remnants of the company are in small scattered groups here and there, laying in behind trees, logs, in shallow foxholes or whatever scant protection there is in the area. We are in a position on the right hand side of the road we came up yesterday, and about 30 yards behind the causeway. I'll try to explain clearly just what happened this morning that has put us where we are now.

All night long there was mortar fire being dropped on us in addition to enemy grenades and plenty of light machine gun fire. During the course of the night, our machine guns were knocked out and many of our automatic rifles, leaving nothing but grenades and rifles to counter fire with, which allowed the enemy to close in on us during the periods of darkness between flares. [With a]ll machine guns out of action, we couldn't spray our front at all hoping to catch the enemy in blind firing. The enemy sensing the fact that we could no longer effect machine gun fire on them kept moving in ready for the kill as soon as the sky began to get light.

One big Nip came at Lieutenant Burke in a banzai charge, bayonet fixed. The lieutenant brought his carbine to his shoulder, sighted in, and "click," the weapon failed to fire. He ejected the cartridge in a split

This low-level reconnaissance photograph was taken from a Navy plane on 16 September and shows details of the two pillboxes that gave the company so much grief during its assaults three days later. Captain Pope did not see this photograph until after the war.
U.S. Marine Corps

Pillbox

Ainsworth's CP

Pillbox

Cannon

★★★★★

second, throwing another into the chamber. As the bolt came forward, [he] sighted in again, and "click." All this time the Nip was getting closer to the lieutenant, "click" went the carbine again, the lieutenant's socks were rolling up and down his trouser legs like window shades (so he says), and he finally threw the carbine at the Nip who was less than ten feet from him. The weapon smacked solidly into the Jap's face, sending the six-foot son of heaven crashing to the ground. Burke was on top of him in a second, and proceeded to punch the arrogant and bleeding face to a pulp, finally being assisted by McAlarnis, who cut the Nip's head off with a nice long burst of a tommy gun.[57]

This is only one of the cases of hand-to-hand combat that took place last night. It was so bad at times that empty grenade boxes, canteens full of water, rocks, and other malfunctioning weapons were hurled at the advancing Nips, each time with satisfactory results. The night was kept illuminated by star shells from ships in the bay, as well as our own mortar batteries.

At about 0005 this morning, I heard someone running and stumbling up the hill toward our CP. Looking over the edge of our position, I recognized the oncomer as a Marine. As he reached our level, he said at the top of his voice, "Lieutenant! Lieutenant Powell! The machine gun on the road is out of action. It won't fire, it's out of action."

"Shut your goddamn big mouth you halfwit," I yelled at him,

---

[57] As we have seen, Sgt McAlarnis's Navy Cross citation describes this episode somewhat differently. From the Navy Cross citation for 2dLt Francis Burke: "Assigned the mission of assaulting Hill 100, a heavily-defended coral nose studded with caves and concrete pillboxes, Second Lieutenant Burke gallantly led his platoon in a furious attack and reached the summit of the hill. Immediately coming under a heavy rifle caliber field piece, which caused numerous casualties, he quickly consolidated the nine remaining men of his platoon into a defense of the forward portion of the hill. Although he received a severe bayonet wound in a hand-to-hand encounter with an enemy soldier, he resolutely remained in his exposed position and continued to lead his men in desperate combat with numerically superior attacking Japanese forces. At dawn, with his automatic weapon out of action, his ammunition exhausted, and his position raked by heavy machine-gun fire, he was ordered to withdraw his men to a new position." How many other acts of heroism during that night went unrecognized since so few men were left alive to record them?

"What the hell do you want to do, invite the Nips over for some of your rations?"

"Well the machine gun is out of action, what'll we do?"

"Get the hell back where you came from and get it fixed. Meanwhile you keep that loose trap of yours tightly shut, chum, or you're very likely to get a posthumous Purple Heart, one way or the other."

Where the lieutenant was I can't say for certain, but if he is still in this CP he has kept silent. 0030 and the lieutenant is definitely in this CP and has started to broadcast the news over the radio that we have a machine gun out of action. I have absolutely given up, but perhaps the Japs' radios are not on our frequency and they will miss the call, however, he can be heard over the entire hill, his fine baritone voice booming out with all the resonance of John Charles Thomas.[58]

It's so light up here when the flares burst that a person could actually read. Come to think of it, I wish I had a good book now. I'd throw it at that blabber-mouthed sergeant. What a war![59]

We maintained radio silence practically all night except when White 6 called us for information occasionally. At about 0115, the skipper called me ever so softly over the radio from his position on the ridge, his voice was almost a whisper. He said, "Top, be sure and keep a sharp lookout on your left flank and left rear. I can see Japs moving down to the left side of the hill and sneaking along the edge of the swamp toward the causeway. They will probably try to get up to within grenade range of your CP. I don't want to open fire because it will give away our positions, so you have your men keep their eyes peeled during the periods between flares. Do you understand all I say?"

---

[58] John Charles Thomas (1891–1960) was a popular baritone known for his booming voice.

[59] After first beginning to narrate the events of the night in the past tense, Ainsworth switches here briefly to the present tense, before returning again to the past, and then back again to the present. In a letter to the Commandant of the Marine Corps, received by Maj Hough on 21 March 1950, Lt R. J. Powell Jr., suggested that it was unclear whether Capt Pope knew that the second platoon of the Recon Company was supporting him. Clearly he did, and just as clearly, that support from below made little difference to him and his beleaguered men on Hill 100.

★★★★★★

"Yes sir," I replied, "I understand, roger out." His set clicked off and I gave the message by word of mouth to Lieutenant Peck, who notified the ten men strung out along the rim of our emplacement as guards.

The remainder of the night was comparatively quiet, but the men were vigilant, never closing their eyes and fully aware that the first signs of daylight would start bringing the Nips down on us in an all-out attack to drive us from the ridge. At 0330 it began to rain, and the wind started to blow, driving the rain through our clothes and chilling to the bone. Some of the men are having chills and there is nothing we can do for them, we don't even have ponchos to keep them warm.[60] Their clothes are still cake stiff with mud from yesterday's sojourn in the swamps, and all-in-all it's damned miserable up here.

I have forgotten to mention an incident that took place about 9 o'clock last night. Possibly it will add a touch of humor to this dirge, although this is a bit ironic. About 9 or 9:30 last night after we had gotten settled down and were waiting for anything to happen, Lieutenant Trout of A Company managed to get over the causeway and up to our positions with a few cases of grenades and some chow and juice for our men. His working party had formed a human chain starting at the bottom, and the supplies are slowly reaching the top.

It's been about three hours since any of us has had a cigarette, and I can't think of anything that would satisfy us more than a few deep inhalations of tobacco smoke, but not a chance. In fact people are so afraid of our position being detected that every time our flares burst overhead we close our eyes to insure against them reflecting the light like a cat's. And what happens? Sergeant Andress, who was also supervising the working party, stopped by our hole in the hill and said in

---

[60] Many of the Guadalcanal veterans of the First Division suffered from continued bouts of malaria.

a rather innocent and sympathetic voice, "Here fellas, here's some smokes," and with that he bolted away under a hail of oaths, curses, and the 15 cartons of Chesterfields he had taken such pains with, getting them here. Again I'm given to say, "what a war."[61]

At 0510 this morning, the first streaks of light in the eastern sky told us that daybreak is just a few minutes away. The Japs are also aware of this and have opened up with their machine guns, at almost point-blank range. They have moved up on us during the night much closer than we had known.

At 0515 the inevitable was here, the Nips, now seeing our flimsy line stretching down the side of the hill, are moving toward the very tip of the nose, where Captain Pope and our left flank are putting up a terrific fight to hurl back the vicious counterattack. Our rifle fire is accurate, and many Japs have gone down under the rapid-fire experts behind the sights, but they are too many for us. We are throwing everything into the attack now. Out of grenades and with no machine guns left, we are throwing boulders, grenade boxes, C rations, and anything else we can get our hands on.

Captain Pope has just radioed me and says that we are going to have to pull out of here right away. [He] asked me to get White 6 on the radio and ask permission to withdraw. I got White 6,[62] and gave him the picture, asking permission to withdraw as the captain had requested.

He answers, "Withdraw to the road at the bottom of the hill."

"Aye, aye, sir."

I switched back to the skipper and gave him the colonel's answer. He replied, "Very well, withdraw immediately, and have your men cover us as we pull out."

---

[61] This episode raises the question of why more was not done to support Charlie Company, since some of these supplies apparently reached the men on the top of Hill 100. Ainsworth's CP was located on the side of the ridge, not far below them.
[62] LtCol Honsowetz.

★★★★★

"Roger, out."[63]

I have told Lieutenants Peck and Schall, and we are now getting out of our night's position and are moving the men down the hill to the road below as quickly as possible. Before we reached the bottom of the hill, the men holding the top of the ridge started to pour down over the nose sliding, stumbling, falling, and recovering enough to turn and fire at the rushing Japs now coming out to the nose of the ridge. The Nip attack is being supported by their machine guns, and tracer bullets are ricocheting off the tip of the nose. They are not yet far enough out on the razorback to be able to fire at those of us now on the road and moving toward the causeway. The Nips are moving their guns up to a point where they will get us in a murderous crossfire if we don't get over the causeway in the next few seconds.

Most of our men are off the hill now and are getting into the edge of the swamp using the causeway for protection. Sergeant McAlarnis is still on the side of the hill making sure that no wounded have been abandoned. The Dead will have to stay.[64]

We are receiving heavy machine gun fire and rifle fire now, and their mortars have also opened up. The tracers are coming across the causeway in a steady stream, looking like liquid fire, and as we reach the other side it looks like we're in for more trouble.

F Company[65] has a machine gun set up at the end of the causeway on the road and 50 feet behind them is a 37 from the weapons company. Right between these two guns is an abandoned Jap truck and under it

---

[63] Although this makes clear that he was granted permission to withdraw, Pope later told an interviewer that he fully expected to be court-martialed by the regimental commander. Lt Powell of the Recon Company wrote in 1950 that his platoon did not receive the order to withdraw until "half an hour" after the departure of Charlie Company from the crest, and that it continued to come under fire from the reoccupied positions on the ridge crest (Hough, 86). His platoon would obviously have seen the men of Charlie Company scrambling down from the top of Hill 100, "ass over teakettle" as Pope would later put it.

[64] The capital letter is 1stSgt Ainsworth's. Their bodies would remain on the ridge until 3 October, when they were finally recovered (Hough, 88).

[65] F/2/1 had been cobbled together with G/2/1 and a squad from the War Dog Platoon to make up a single skeleton company (Hough, 84).

are two figures, just what color we can't make out. Our withdrawal is held up momentarily while we try to identify these two characters. We are pleading to them in a manner becoming a Marine, with such phrases as "For Christ's sake don't shoot, we're Marines," and "Hold your fire cobbers, we're C Company."

Suddenly Corporal [Warren R.] Curtiss[66] yells out, "Those bastards are Japs, hit the deck, here comes a grenade."

Damned if it didn't.

WHAM! Off it goes, and Curtiss is up in a flash firing his weapon at the two yellow men who damn near accomplished their mission of bottling us up from both ends. But they didn't, and what is left of the company is behind Fox Company lines trying to organize some kind of a secondary defense. I doubt very much that the Nips will try to run us out of here with manpower and bayonet charges, they wouldn't get to first base as the causeway is now sufficiently covered by machine guns, and the 37 that is pointed directly down its middle.

We have given up the ridge because of lack of support by our present commander.[67] We started this attack yesterday with little of anything and have ended up with less, after what I shall call the most stubborn, determined holding action yet witnessed in any battle yet fought on this island and probably the Pacific. The last is a broad statement, but I want to hear of any outfit who under the same conditions has done any better, and until I do, what I've already said still goes. I only wish that Major Stevenson could have been there with us or could have watched his old company perform. I'm sure he would have been proud of the guys he skippered for so long.[68] I know there has never been a first sergeant as proud of his company as I am of this one. They have shown a spirit of fight and determination unsurpassed in the division, with the poorest exhibition of support I've ever seen. We've lost the ridge, but we've lost it honorably. No man is ashamed.

---

[66] Curtiss had already been wounded.
[67] LtCol Honsowetz.
[68] Maj Stevenson commanded C/1/1 before Capt Pope.

★★★★★★

It comes to me now that F Company could have very effectively covered our withdrawal, yet they didn't so much as fire a shot. And how is it that the two Japs managed to get in under the truck in the 50-foot space between their machine gun and the 37mm pointing down the causeway? I remember now that as I passed their machine gun in our withdrawal, the entire crew were sitting there with their mouths hanging open taking in the show. This was one of the numerous instances of non-support I have spoken of. So here we are, more killed, more wounded, trying to reorganize for anything, or any orders to attack again. Attack again, that's rich! With what?[69]

There are roughly 15 of us in this immediate area, many helping take the wounded back. There are no stretchers available, no stretcher bearers. Mortars continue to drop in the area, and we are keeping low in our holes. Lieutenant Burke, Sergeant McAlarnis, and myself are trying to find enough men to build up a good line of defense, but it's impossible. The most we can muster is about 25, so we are holding on and awaiting orders. I am going back to see White 6 and give him the picture, maybe Captain Pope is back there and getting some dope.

It is now 0632 and I am at the rear command post. I have just finished talking to the CO-LT-21.[70] He tells me that Charlie Company is to attack again at 0800. Arguing with him gained nothing. He does not seem to understand that there is no more Charlie Company. He tells me that in this attack we will clean out the ravine between the ridge we just lost and the one on its left.

It's suicide, nothing less. I can't make him see that the most we can muster is about 25 men, and over half of those are without weapons, ammunition, and need food and water. We have the fight, but we've nothing to fight with. We will attack at 0800.

I'm on the way back to give Lieutenant Burke the news. We have

---

[69] These recriminations were unfair since F Company had suffered badly itself, but understandable in the circumstances.
[70] LtCol Honsowetz.

only about one hour before we attack unless something can be done by Major Davis.[71] I think if our executive officer[72] knew what was up in the air he would damn sure do something about it. Rank doesn't scare him in the least, and the man who is in command of us at present is fighting to the last man in the 1st Battalion.

Back with Lieutenant Burke and the rest of the men, I told them what my trip had accomplished and the bad news, "the Attack Order." It was accepted without comment, but the bewildered expressions on the faces of these gallant Marines told what they had on their minds. They wandered back to their holes, lit cigarettes, some of them inhaling deeply, pushing their helmets back on their heads, and with an air of nonchalance and disgust, relaxed, emitting long sighs, exhaling the blue smoke skyward. Few of them talk. Those who did, talked of the man in

---

[71] Maj Ray Davis was the commanding officer of 1/1. In his oral biography, Pope indicated that he believed that it was the intervention of Davis that caused this absurd order to be rescinded. There is a discrepancy with regard to the timing of this between the narrative of 1stSgt Ainsworth and the official history of the 1st Battalion, but the essential facts are the same. The official history, which dates to November 1944, states that: "At 1630, C.O. LT 21 ordered C Company to attack up the deep ravine between the ridge they had just lost and another ridge to the left (West). Capt Pope contacted C.O. LT 1/1 [Maj Davis] and reported only 15 men and two officers able to attack. The attack order was rescinded." I am inclined to believe that Ainsworth's contemporary narrative is authoritative. His version of the order is virtually identical to the one given in the official history, but it is likely that this all took place in the morning, as he describes, rather than in the afternoon, as the official version indicates. As he notes below, by the early afternoon of 20 September, the remnants of C Company had already been withdrawn some 2,000 yards from the front lines. The story is in any case the same in all versions: the CO of 2/1 issued the order, and Maj Davis of 1/1 had it rescinded. Pope may have been briefly out of action during the morning. Later he credited Davis for intervening to save his life and the lives of the survivors of Charlie Company. In a 1998 communication to Jon Hoffmann, Pope wrote: "After we came down, I called forward our few remaining mortarmen, who had been firing during the night to protect us. They joined us (without their tubes) and this brought our total to about 13 to 15. There were also some walking wounded, including me. A young second lieutenant named Schall had been with our mortar platoon, and was instantly killed while, standing by my side, I advised him of our orders. The movement up Hill 100 was then delayed for a few minutes when the men asked me to find a corpsman to go with us. This delay allowed an officer-messenger to reach me with orders canceling the attack. I will never forget those 15 or so men, knowing that they were about to die, preparing to attack Hill 100 again." The following day the battered 1st Marines were withdrawn at the insistence of MajGen Geiger, over the objections of both Puller and Rupertus.

[72] Maj Stevenson.

charge of us, who they knew was sending us into what would prove fatal to the men of Charlie Company who remained.

Private First Class John J. Maguire has located a machine gun somewhere and is setting it up on the edge of the swamp. Some of the men are in search of some belted ammunition and if they are lucky we will have added a little more firepower to the lines.

The time is now 0732, and the time for the new attack is but a few minutes off. The men have found the ammunition for our latest addition, the machine gun, and they're popping away furiously at the top of the ridge, its value being only harassing. It will keep those yellow heads down, and perhaps give someone a chance to advance. Who it might be, I can't say. I do know definitely who it won't be, and that is the bunch of Boy Scouts who comprise the front lines at present. They've been there the better part of the night and all morning, and it looks as if they intend staying there until that ridge is finally secured at someone else's expense. It is truly pathetic to look around and see what is left of the company, so few and yet with such fighting hearts.

It is 0754, and word has been sent up for Charlie Company to withdraw, we are being relieved this afternoon by fresh troops of the 7th Marines. Lieutenant Burke spoke but two words upon hearing this news: "Thank God."

It is now 0845 and the proposed attack started on schedule, but was called off at 0830. The entire 1st Battalion is being pulled out of the fight for a rest. At 1332, we are in an area about 2,000 yards in rear of the lines, waiting for the 7th Marines to arrive and take over. The 2d Battalion may not be so fortunate. We are having hot chow tonight, and although the men all thought they would be hungry enough to go for second helpings, the majority were barely able to finish the generous portion handed them on the initial trip through the chow line. All however had second or third cups of coffee.

Our day is coming to a close now, and as I sit here against a stump of coconut tree, I am thinking over everything that has happened since the day we landed here in what we were told would be a fast decisive battle ending in our favor after not more than two or three days at most. Today ends our sixth day of the battle for Peleliu, and the area that is now controlled by the whole division is a mere fraction of this tiny three-by-five island that has cost so much this far to take. I've been thinking of the deeds of valor done by these men who now lie around in little groups and individuals alike, smoking, talking over last night's battles, and inquiring of each other just what they think will come next. So many heroic achievements accomplished by groups and individuals alike that one cannot give praise to just this one and that one, for every man of the company has shown a devotion to duty and such complete disregard for their own safety in displays of heroism and intrepidity in action, that to name one for outstanding performance in battle would be showing a marked partiality. Every man in Charlie Company was outstanding during every battle thus far in the campaign.

A wounded Marine gets a drink of water from a buddy's canteen while awaiting
stretcher bearers. The scorching 100-plus degree temperatures and humidity proved
nearly as tough a foe as the heavily entrenched Japanese.
Headquarters U.S. Marine Corps 94986

POSTSCRIPT

Here, Ainsworth's narrative comes to an abrupt end. Nine lines on the top of the last page of the typescript are unreadable. The last paragraph appears to have been typed twice on the page, using carbon paper. The last words on the page, after "campaign," are "Never has . . . ," and it is not difficult to reconstruct what he was going to write.

According to the history of the 1st Battalion, sent to the commanding officer of the 1st Marines on 23 November 1944 when memories were still fresh, the survivors of Charlie Company continued to be engaged even after their withdrawal from the front lines. Thus on 22 September, D+7, the company "exchanged grenades with Japs most of the night," and Sergeant McAlarnis was wounded and evacuated "under protest." On 25 September, D+10, the battalion history records that "20 Japs were killed by C Company machine gun fire on the reef . . . while trying to leave Peleliu," and that on D+14, "C Company, with the aid of an amphibious tractor, sent a patrol to the reef 600 yards east of the north end of Peleliu and wiped out a Japanese position there, killing 184 Japs and taking one prisoner." Presumably these Japanese were also trying to escape; in the circumstances, it is understandable that they were given no quarter. Finally, on 4 October, after what must have been an uncomfortable night on an LST, the survivors of Charlie Company embarked on the USS *Tryon* (APH 1) for Pavuvu, arriving there on 10 October.[73] Fifteen officers and 363 men remained of the 1st Battalion's

---

[73] Eric Mailander's tally of official casualties for C Company shows that 74 percent were either killed or wounded by 20 September. The rifle platoons suffered 82 percent casualties and every NCO and officer was hit, including Capt Pope and 1stSgt Ainsworth. (Both men were able to return to duty on the same day.)

complement of some 1,300. The battalion history makes a point of noting that Captain Pope was the only one of the original rifle company commanders left. On the transport and back at the base camp of Pavuvu, he and First Sergeant Ainsworth would have been occupied with writing letters to the families of the men who had died.

Jack Ainsworth was discharged with the rank of Sergeant Major in 1946. He remained in the reserves until 1948, but his life thereafter is mostly a mystery. His next of kin during the war is listed as a wife, Virginia, but later, in San Francisco in 1971, he married a graduate of Vassar College. She was 12 years younger, and the marriage lasted only a few months. Ainsworth died in San Francisco at the age of 64 in 1981, from, according to the death certificate, the consequences of alcoholism. He was disabled, a quadriplegic, and his death was reported by a friend. There is no mention on the death certificate of family or occupation, much less of the fact that he was a highly-decorated veteran. There was no memorial service or obituary for the Silver Star recipient.

As for his skipper, Everett Pope lived a productive and for the most part, a happy life. While still in his early thirties, he became president of a Boston cooperative bank. He and his wife Eleanor were married for 65 years, and they had two sons and two granddaughters. After his retirement from banking, he served as chairman of the board of trustees of Bowdoin College, and led an effort to raise a memorial on the Bowdoin campus to the dead of World War II, Korea, and Vietnam. It is an understated affair in New England granite. One of the names etched on it is that of Captain Andrew Haldane, his Bowdoin classmate, who died on Peleliu.

In a 1996 oral history interview with Benis Frank of the USMC History Division, my father maintained that he had been unaffected psychologically by what he had experienced. But the cocky young Marine in the jungle of Cape Gloucester who grins out at the camera is not the same man as the father I knew and loved. It is unlikely that any of the men who fought at Peleliu were ever quite the same again.

Everett Pope died on his 90th birthday, on 16 July 2009, and is buried at Arlington National Cemetery.

Capt Everett Pope on Cape Gloucester, 1944
Courtesy of Ambassador Laurence Pope